The
PREPPER'S
COOKBOOK

Essential Prepping Foods and Recipes
to Deliciously Survive Any Disaster

Rockridge Press

Copyright © 2013 by Rockridge Press, Berkeley, California

No part of this publication may be reproduced, stored in a retrieval system or transmitted in any form or by any means, electronic, mechanical, photocopying, recording, scanning or otherwise, except as permitted under Sections 107 or 108 of the 1976 United States Copyright Act, without the prior written permission of the Publisher. Requests to the Publisher for permission should be addressed to the Permissions Department, Rockridge Press, 918 Parker St, Suite A-12, Berkeley, CA 94710.

Limit of Liability/Disclaimer of Warranty: The Publisher and the author make no representations or warranties with respect to the accuracy or completeness of the contents of this work and specifically disclaim all warranties, including without limitation warranties of fitness for a particular purpose. No warranty may be created or extended by sales or promotional materials. The advice and strategies contained herein may not be suitable for every situation. This work is sold with the understanding that the publisher is not engaged in rendering medical, legal or other professional advice or services. If professional assistance is required, the services of a competent professional person should be sought. Neither the Publisher nor the author shall be liable for damages arising herefrom. The fact that an individual, organization or website is referred to in this work as a citation and/or potential source of further information does not mean that the author or the Publisher endorses the information the individual, organization or website may provide or recommendations they/it may make. Further, readers should be aware that Internet websites listed in this work may have changed or disappeared between when this work was written and when it is read.

For general information on our other products and services or to obtain technical support, please contact our Customer Care Department within the U.S. at (866) 744-2665, or outside the U.S. at (510) 253-0500.

Rockridge Press publishes its books in a variety of electronic and print formats. Some content that appears in print may not be available in electronic books, and vice versa.

TRADEMARKS: Rockridge Press and the Rockridge Press logo are trademarks or registered trademarks of Callisto Media Inc. and/or its affiliates, in the United States and other countries, and may not be used without written permission. All other trademarks are the property of their respective owners. Rockridge Press is not associated with any product or vendor mentioned in this book.

ISBN: Print 978-1-62315-197-3 | eBook 978-1-62315-198-0

CONTENTS

INTRODUCTION: WHY PREP?

Regardless of what reality TV would have you believe, preppers aren't paranoid people rushing around gathering food in underground bunkers and spouting conspiracy theories. Most are real-world people just like you, who simply want to be prepared to survive any emergency that may arise. These emergencies include natural disasters such as hurricanes or blizzards, as well as global emergencies such as economic collapse or war. For that matter, what if you simply lose your job and don't have grocery money? If you have food stored away, your family won't go hungry during those lean weeks.

Stocking enough food in advance is practical, too. When news of an emergency such as a hurricane or blizzard is announced, people rush to the store and clean the shelves. If you're at work or otherwise unable to get to the store, there may be nothing left by the time you get there. If you stock up in advance, you don't have to worry about any of that, because you're already prepared.

There are several different ways to build an emergency food supply, including buying canned and dry goods, canning your own food, and dehydrating products. This book will teach you how to stock your pantry using a combination of these methods.

Keep in mind that you may not have modern conveniences such as electricity, running water, cell towers, or road access during an emergency. Prepare as if you're going on a backwoods camping trip.

Why Create Home-Prepped Food?

Home canning and dehydrating are great ways to build an emergency food supply with a minimal investment. The best part is that you can prepare your own delicious, nutritious recipes instead of relying on tasteless, chemical-laden, commercially canned foods. It's also significantly cheaper to can your own foods, after the initial equipment investment.

Two huge advantages to making your own food include the fact that you'll know every single ingredient that goes into your recipes, and although most commercial products have a two-year marked shelf life, your products will retain their edibility and nutritional value for many years. As a matter of fact, there are documented cases of people eating food 100 years after it was canned. Although certainly not recommended, it goes to show that if you do it right, your food will last.

A Quick Start to Prepping

The following short checklist is to get you thinking about your emergency-preparedness plan. While the focus of this book is preparing stores of food for emergencies, this list will help you with your overall planning. At the back of the book, also see a checklist for a bug-out bag. Bug-out bags, discussed in more detail in Chapter 1, contain small amounts of food and supplies for quick get-aways.

Prepper's Checklist — Getting Started

- ☐ Avoid foods with lots of salt because the excess sodium will make you thirsty.
- ☐ Include a variety of foods in order to meet your nutritional and caloric needs.
- ☐ Have ready-to-eat foods on hand to conserve your fuel and water.
- ☐ Keep a manual can opener near your food supply.
- ☐ Store at least 3 days' worth of food per family member.
- ☐ Store 1 gallon of water a day per person for both drinking and sanitation.
- ☐ Keep your prescription medication handy.
- ☐ Have some portable food on hand in case you need to leave your house in a hurry.
- ☐ Don't forget food for your pet.
- ☐ See the back of the book for a bug-out bag checklist.

These basic points will help you start building your emergency food supply. The next section focuses on different food-preservation methods and how to properly use each. You'll also find some great recipes to get you started.

Preparing Your Supplies and Food Stores

1

GETTING STARTED: FOOD PREPPING 101

As already discussed, you may not have access to modern amenities during an emergency, so you're going to need food that's been preserved in a manner that doesn't depend on refrigeration or possibly even cooking. There are several different ways that you can do this, and this chapter previews some of the most popular and successful methods of food preparation and cooking featured throughout this book.

Alternative Cooking Methods

Many of the foods that you're going to prepare are ready to eat, but if the emergency event extends beyond a day or two, you'll get pretty tired of cold food. Also, if you're a coffee drinker or a person who likes to wash in warm water, you'll probably want to have a heat source handy that doesn't require electricity. There are several options out there, and all of them have their ups and downs. It is best to have more than one cooking method available, just in case.

Open Wood Fires

Without a doubt, this is the most popular way to cook without power, especially if you need an alternative source of heat for more than a day or two. If you plan to cook over an open fire, you can either use a campfire-type pit or you can build a fire pit that already has racks, a flue, and whatever other accessories you'd like to build into it.

If you decide to cook with wood, you'll need to have a plentiful stock of dried wood and a way to light it. Wet wood won't burn and it will create an excessive amount of smoke that can affect the flavor of your food. Also, you can only use it outside, so plan to cook in all weather conditions if this is one of your methods.

Tools that you'll need:

- Wood
- Rocks
- Rack, tripod, or special cooking rack with legs
- Iron skillets, a Dutch oven, iron or copper kettles, or any combination of these
- Wooden or metal spoons and spatulas with longer handles
- Pot holders or towels to move your cookware
- Cast iron or other metal fire poker or wooden stick

Prep Tip

If you use your skillets over an open fire, smear some liquid dish soap on the bottom and outside first. The black carbon from the fire will wipe right off when you wash the skillet.

Barbecue Grill

You can always use your barbecue grill to cook with. Stock up on charcoal or fuel, and as with an open fire, be prepared to cook in inclement weather. The downside here is that fuel supplies are limited to what you store, although you can always burn wood in it if you run out of charcoal or propane. If you opt to do this, though, make sure you remove the fuel tanks completely prior to building a wood or charcoal fire in your gas grill.

Supplies that you'll need:

- Fire starter if you're using charcoal or wood
- Fuel
- Barbecue utensils
- Skillets, Dutch ovens, pots, or a combination of these to cook foods that you can't prepare on the racks

Fireplace or Wood-Burning Stove

The advantages to using your fireplace or wood-burning cookstove as an alternative cooking method are many. The biggest two advantages probably are that you can cook inside in any weather and that as long as you have wood, you have a fuel source. However, if it's hot outside, your house is going to become really hot from the residual heat. You'll need the same equipment that you'd need for cooking on a campfire.

Camp Stove

The advantage to using a camp stove is that it's portable. If you need to leave in a hurry, you have a heat source that you can toss in the car or strap to your bug-out bag without adding much weight. The downsides are that you need fuel for it and you can't use it indoors. Expect to get about an hour of heat from a 16.4-ounce fuel bottle.

Solar Oven

A solar oven consists of solar panels and a black pot that holds your food. The solar panels trap the heat and direct it to the pot. It doesn't require any fuel other than the sun, but if it's a cold or overcast day, it won't be effective enough to cook with.

Rocket Stove

A rocket stove is a small, single-burner stove that uses wood to efficiently trap heat in a high-temperature combustion chamber. The smaller ones are portable, but you'll need wood to fuel them.

Volcano Stove

These are wonderful gadgets to keep in your emergency kit because they're light, portable, self-contained, and extremely efficient. You can use wood, charcoal, or propane, and many of them already have racks on them. The concept is that the heat is funneled directly to the food instead of being lost to the environment.

Stove in a Can

These amazing little tools are lightweight and easy to throw into your bug-out bag or emergency kit. They're simply little heat cells that you place in the bottom of a can to convert it into a stove.

Prep Tip

Don't use a charcoal grill or other cooking devices within enclosed areas. The toxic carbon monoxide they produce can build up without you knowing it (it's colorless and odorless).

Alternative Food Sources

There are several different sources from which you can gather food-stuffs for your emergency food supply, but the most important thing to remember is that you need to rotate your emergency food supply. The best way to do that is to use your emergency supply as part of your usual food stores. You shouldn't be stocking your pantry with foods that you wouldn't eat anyway; make your emergency supply a larger version of what you already buy, with perhaps just a little more emphasis on canned proteins such as tuna and chicken.

One thing that you'll need to remember, however, is the idea that sugar and excess calories are always bad. In an emergency situation, you're going to need calorie-dense foods in order to meet your energy requirements, because you may not be eating three to five low-calorie meals per day. You may need to get all of your energy from one or two food bars.

The Value of Condiments

Imagine how much easier it would be to live on canned chicken for a week if you had some mayonnaise, canned gravy, mustard, teriyaki sauce, and maybe some pickle relish. Condiments can make all of the difference in the world and they're cheap. They will also be great barter items because everybody is going to be sick of eating plain meat and vegetables. Seasonings will also make your life easier and will be valuable, so don't forget them when you're building your stockpile.

Commercially Preserved Foods

The idea of starting your supply may seem daunting, but it's actually quite easy. Just buy a little bit extra each time that you go to the store.

It doesn't even have to be much. Start with buying two cans of chicken broth or tuna instead of one. It's that easy; but of course, if you can buy more, then your supply would build faster.

Be careful when you buy commercially canned or boxed foods because they're often full of salt and preservatives. Also, remember that you can't go by the serving size listed on the can or box. You know your appetite and that of your family. If each of you can eat a can of tuna, then use an entire can as one serving when you're doing your planning.

If you use coupons and take advantage of buy-one-get-one-free sales at the grocery store, you can build your emergency supply fairly inexpensively and quickly.

Meals Ready to Eat (MREs)

Originally created by the military, these are vacuum-packed meals that are ready to eat right out of the package. These can range from single-food meals such as green beans to full meals such as lasagna. In recent years, technology has even advanced to the point where these meals heat themselves via a chemical reaction with just a few spoonfuls of water dropped in the outside layer of the pack. These are great for your bug-out bag because they're light and generally packed with nutrients and calories.

Meal-Replacement Bars

You've seen them in the supermarkets and convenience stores, and you've probably even had at least one meal-replacement bar in your life. They're a great food for your bug-out bag because they're portable, macronutrient-rich, and easy to eat on the run. They also don't weigh much or take up much space. As with all processed foods, watch the sodium content so they don't make you thirsty.

Home-Canned Foods

Preserving foods via canning has been practiced for centuries, and it simply involves heating the food to a temperature that kills all harmful bacteria and pushes air out of the jar so that harmful bacteria can't grow inside of the jar. There are three primary ways to can foods: water bath (or boiling water) canning, pressure canning, and dry canning. The first two are by far the most common, but all three methods are reviewed in this book, accompanied by some fabulous recipes.

Dehydrated Foods

This process involves removing the water from produce and meats to greatly reduce the rate of spoilage. Once the water is out of the food, it can be dry-canned or vacuum-packed and kept for years without losing much of the nutritional value. You can dehydrate foods fairly easily at home using a food dehydrator that costs very little. But try to get one with heat settings so you can dry foods at the temperatures recommended for best results. Dehydrated foods can be rehydrated in a few hours by soaking the food in water or another liquid.

Freeze-Dried Foods

This is a fairly expensive process because of the equipment required, so most people just buy freeze-dried foods. It involves instantly flash-freezing the food so it remains in basically the same nutritional state that it was in prior to being freeze-dried. You lose very little of the nutritional value when you freeze-dry food.

Vacuum-Packed Foods

Vacuum-packing involves sealing a food product in plastic that has had all of the air sucked out of it. Spoilage can still occur, however, and if a food required refrigeration prior to being vacuum-packed, it will still need to be refrigerated after vacuum-packing.

These are the most common methods of preparing foods for long-term storage. Canning and dehydrating will be discussed more in depth over the next several chapters.

Building Your Bug-Out Bag

If your house was on fire, a flood was coming, or another event requiring you to leave quickly occurred, wouldn't it be good to have all of your important documents and some emergency items altogether in one spot where you could quickly grab them? Of course it would, and that's exactly what a bug-out bag is: a bag that's already packed with vital items and a small supply of food in case you need to "bug out" in a hurry. You may hear this emergency bag referred to by the following names:

- 72-hour bag
- GOOD (Get out of Dodge) bag
- Go bag
- PERK (Personal Emergency Relocation Kit) bag

Regardless of what you call it, there are many different reasons to pack one. The idea originated with military personnel who were accustomed to being called out in a hurry and has been adopted by civilians who believe in being prepared.

How Do You Decide What to Put in Your Bug-Out Bag?

What food goes in your bug-out bag depends upon several factors, including:

- What type of event you're preparing for
- Who's going to carry it
- How far it will be carried
- Where you're going to store it
- Geographical needs

Regardless of these factors, several items should be in every bug-out bag. See the back of the book for a bug-out bag checklist that includes food, water, and some standard items that should be in every bag, plus some optional items such as medications, blankets, pet food, and maps.

2

DECIDING HOW MUCH FOOD
AND WATER YOU'LL NEED

B uilding your emergency food and water supply may seem like a daunting task, but it doesn't have to be. The best way to begin is to ask yourself how many people will be using the supplies when an emergency happens. Government sources such as the Federal Emergency Management Agency (FEMA) and most state disaster-preparedness departments recommend a minimum three-day supply of food and water. A week's worth is a safer estimate, especially if you live in a disaster-prone tornado, earthquake, blizzard, or hurricane area. The following guidelines will help you create a plan.

Calorie Guidelines

When you look at commercially prepared food, you've surely noticed that there are serving sizes indicated on the containers. You may also have noticed that those servings are often small. If you base your emergency food supply estimations on those serving sizes, you will run out of food faster than expected. Instead, base your stockpile on caloric needs. See the following table for suggested caloric needs. If you need 2,000 calories, your significant other needs 2,000 calories, and your child needs 1,200 calories, then you need to store at least 5,200 calories worth of food per day.

	AGE	SEDENTARY	MODERATELY ACTIVE	ACTIVE
Child (female and male)	2 – 3	1,000 – 1,200	1,000 – 1,400	1,000 – 1,400
Female	4 – 8	1,200 – 1,400	1,400 – 1,600	1,400 – 1,800
	9 – 13	1,400 – 1,600	1,600 – 2,000	1,800 – 2,200
	14 – 18	1,800	2,000	2,400
	19 – 30	1,800 – 2,000	2,000 – 2,200	2,400
	31 – 50	1,800	2,000	2,200
	51 +	1,600	1,800	2,000 – 2,200
Male	4 – 8	1,200 – 1,400	1,400 – 1,600	1,600 – 2,000
	9 – 13	1,600 – 2,000	1,800 – 2,200	2,000 – 2,600
	14 – 18	2,000 – 2,400	2,400 – 2,800	2,800 – 3,200
	19 – 30	2,400 – 2,600	2,600 – 2,800	3,000
	31 – 50	2,200 – 2,400	2,400 – 2,600	2,800 – 3,000
	51 +	2,000 – 2,200	2,200 – 2,400	2,400 – 2,800

Macronutrient Guidelines

When planning your daily caloric needs, be sure to do so with one eye on your macronutrient needs to maintain proper nutrition. That sounds all well and good, but the term *macronutrients* sounds pretty complicated, right? It's actually quite simple, though. Macronutrients are just the major nutrients that your body needs to function properly and thrive.

There are five categories of macronutrients: protein, fat, fiber, carbohydrate, and water, and you need them in certain ratios to remain healthy. Fiber and water are independent nutrients, but protein, fat, and carbs work together to keep you healthy. The table below shows the proper protein, fat, and carb intake percentages for your family.

AGE	PROTEIN	FAT	CARBOHYDRATES
Young children (1 - 3 years)	5 - 20%	30 - 40%	45 - 65%
Older children (4 - 18 years)	10 - 30%	25 - 35%	45 - 65%
Adults (19 years and older)	10 - 35%	20 - 35%	45 - 65%

Prep Tip

When building your food stockpile, make sure to store a variety of foods. There's a phenomenon called food fatigue in which your body becomes sick from constantly eating too much of limited kinds of food.

Water Guidelines

You need to drink at least 64 ounces of water per day and include between 20 and 40 grams of fiber per day in your diet, as well. Kids need a little bit less water. Use the following good rule of thumb when determining how much water your body really needs: half of your body weight in ounces. In other words, if you weigh 180 pounds, half of that is 90. You should drink at least 90 ounces of water per day to preserve proper hydration. At a minimum, keep 1 gallon of water on hand per person, per day for both drinking and sanitation needs. Remember: you can live for up to three weeks without food. Without water, you'll die in a matter of days. Water storage and purification will be covered in Chapter 2.

Additional Store-Bought Foods

Although making your own emergency food based on the delicious recipes in this book is recommended—they are more flavorful and cheaper in the long run—you can begin building your supplies immediately with store-bought foods. Once you begin making your own canned and dehydrated foods, swap these items out. Note that many of the items in this list do not have a long shelf life. Check the best-by dates regularly (it's recommended you do this every 3 months).

- Baking and pancake mixes
- Baking powder, yeast, and baking soda
- Bouillon cubes or powder
- Boxed potatoes
- Canned beans
- Canned fruits, fruit juices, and vegetables
- Canned meat, chili, and soup
- Canned nuts
- Crackers
- Dried beans
- Dried corn
- Dried fruit
- Dry pasta
- Evaporated milk
- Fruit juices and sports drinks
- Granola and sports bars
- Instant coffee, tea, and cocoa
- Jams and jellies
- Peanut butter

- Powdered milk
- Ready-to-eat cereals and uncooked instant cereals
- Salt and other spices
- Sugar, honey, or molasses
- Vegetable oil or shortening
- Vitamins and mineral supplements
- Wheat or other flour (for bread making)
- White rice

Meal Planner

Use the following table to plan the meals and water you and your family will need for one week.

	Breakfast	Lunch	Dinner	Water
Monday				
Tuesday				
Wednesday				
Thursday				

	Breakfast	Lunch	Dinner	Water
Friday				
Saturday				
Sunday				

3

WATER STORAGE AND PURIFICATION

Regardless of what is going on around you, you won't be able to survive for long without clean, potable water. In fact, after just 24 hours without water, your brain stops functioning properly, and within three days, your organs will start to fail. In less than a week, you'll be dead. Water doesn't just keep your tissues hydrated, it also:

- Carries waste and toxins out of your body
- Helps keep your body temperature normal and regular
- Keeps your joints lubricated
- Keeps your blood liquid so it can carry oxygen and nutrients throughout your body
- Aids with digestion
- Keeps your eyes lubricated and healthy
- Keeps your brain functioning properly

In a nutshell, water keeps you alive and you have to have it.

Finding and Gathering Safe Drinking Water

One of the first steps to emergency preparedness is finding a viable source of water. Unfortunately, after certain disasters such as earthquakes, hurricanes, or floods, sources of water that were once safe to drink may no longer be, so you need to have backup plans.

Finding Viable Sources of Water Locally

If you had to name five sources of fresh water within a five-mile radius, would you be able to do it? It seems easy, but many people struggle with it because they simply don't take the time to familiarize themselves with their surroundings. Just knowing where to find water in an emergency situation is going to give you an advantage over many of your peers, and it can be quite enjoyable, too!

Field trips are always fun and are a great way to take your family out and learn about your surrounding area. Make it fun. If you have kids, do a scavenger hunt or go camping. If you don't, make it a hiking trip or picnic with friends or significant others. Make a map with distances marked, because five minutes in a car is actually quite a distance when you're on foot. Some of the best sources for fresh water include:

- Rivers
- Streams
- Retention ponds (Make sure it's not a wastewater pond!)
- Lakes
- Springs
- Natural ponds
- Wells

It's important to know the difference between fresh water, wastewater, brackish water, and salt water because only the freshwater is really useful as a water source. Wastewater is no good for drinking for obvious reasons, and brackish or salt water can actually kill you by dehydration because of the salt in it . . . although it may be okay for such things as flushing toilets.

Wells are actually great because they're generally built over an underground stream or spring and are thus a self-replenishing source of water. As a matter of fact, it's not a bad idea to have a well dug on your property, or make that something you look for when you're searching properties.

Rainwater

Rainwater is another great source of potable water and can be captured in many different ways. Perhaps the easiest ways are to just use buckets or barrels, or to hang a tarp to capture it and then drain the tarp into your barrels. There are also capture systems that you can buy that actually purify water as it's captured. As a matter of fact, you can use these systems for your home as a natural water source instead of depending upon your local water company to provide chemically treated water for a price.

Like all of your other supplies, rotate your rainwater supply so it stays fresh. Even if you don't have a rainwater purification system to use the water in the house, it's great to use outside for watering your plants, bathing, filling the pool, or doing outside chores such as washing windows.

Bottled Water

In addition to knowing where to find a ready supply of fresh water for long-term use, it's a good idea to store bottled water as well. Many people store only enough for a few days or a week because of the amount of space it takes up. Plan for at least one gallon of water per person, per day, and that's just for drinking and cooking purposes. If you're going to plan for hygiene uses as well, double that to two gallons of water per person, per day. Here are some options that you have for storing water:

- Commercially bottled water in personal-sized bottles
- Commercially bottled water in gallon bottles or larger containers
- Home-bottled tap water, purified
- Home-bottled rainwater, purified
- It's fine to bottle water from the tap or from your home filtering system, but make sure that it's purified before you store it so that bacteria can't grow in it. Rotate your water stocks just like you rotate your foods. Use it naturally and replenish regularly.

Water Purification Methods

During an emergency event such as a hurricane, flood, earthquake, or tornado, even the purest sources of water may become unsafe to drink. The best way to ensure that your water is drinkable is to purify it yourself prior to drinking it, if it's not in a bottle. Not only do you need to know how to do it, you need to teach each member of your family how to make water safe, too.

Mechanical Filtration

The water filters in refrigerators use mechanical filtration. This method involves running your water through filters such as sand, charcoal, ceramic, or silver to remove debris and physical contaminants.

If you'd like to make your own filtration system at home, you can do so fairly easily. Here's what you'll need:

- 2-liter soda bottle, cut in half
- Coffee filter, cheesecloth, paper towel, or other cloth-type filtering material
- ½ cup sand
- ½ cup charcoal
- 1 cup gravel

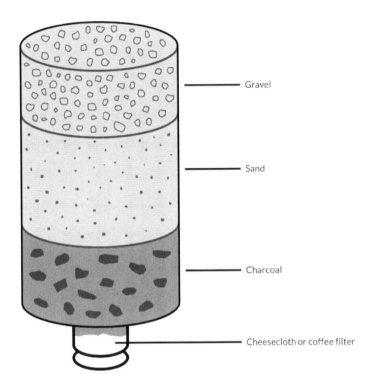

Flip the top half of the soda bottle upside down into the bottom half of the bottle so that the mouth of the bottle is facing down like a funnel. Put the filter either inside the "funnel" part of the bottle or secure it with a rubber band or string on the outside of the spout. Place the charcoal inside first. Then place the sand on top of the charcoal followed by the gravel. Simply pour the dirty water over the gravel so that it filters down through the rocks, charcoal, and sand, and then drips into the bottom half of the bottle.

Add the water slowly so that it stays below the top of the filter. Otherwise the dirty water will run down the outside of the filter. Remember also that this method filters out only debris; it doesn't kill pathogens or parasites, so you may want to use a chemical treatment after you filter it.

Boiling

The age-old, tried-and-true method of purifying water is to boil it. If your municipal water supply is compromised, local officials will issue a "boil water" advisory that instructs you to boil your water for 3 to 12 minutes prior to drinking to kill pathogens. Unless you live at an extremely high elevation, 5 minutes at a rolling boil is long enough to purify the water.

There are two downsides to boiling water: it doesn't filter out physical contaminants and it uses a tremendous amount of fuel if you're heating with bottled gas or other finite sources of heat. To help minimize the impact on your fuel supply, boil your water while you're cooking meals.

Pasteurization

You probably associate pasteurization with milk or juice products, but it's actually just a fancy name for heating a liquid to 160 degrees F for at least 6 minutes to kill pathogens and other bad "bugs" in a liquid. It works equally as well for water as it does for milk and juice, and uses much less fuel than boiling water for several minutes. There are actually solar products that will heat your water to this temperature; if you use one of those methods, you won't waste any fuel at all. As with boiling, pasteurization doesn't remove debris, so you may still want to filter your water before you pasteurize it.

Distillation

This process is pretty complicated, but it produces water that's extremely clean. To distill your water, you will boil it in an enclosed container that has a hose that allows the steam to escape. The steam then converts back into clean water that collects in another container, leaving the impurities behind.

Chlorine Bleach

Plain old household bleach (sodium hypochlorite) is your best friend in an emergency situation. It quite literally kills everything that could possibly harm you in water or on surfaces, and it's dirt cheap. Simply add ¼ teaspoon to a gallon of water, and give it 30 minutes or so to work and your water is good to go. Use unscented bleach, and change it out every six months or so because it does degrade and lose its effectiveness.

Calcium Hypochlorite, aka Pool Shock

The same stuff that people use to keep their pools clean and clear will do the same for your drinking water, and it's extremely affordable. Unlike bleach, it doesn't degrade, and a five-dollar bag will purify about 10,000 gallons of water. There are several different kinds and strengths, so you need to read the label carefully when you're buying it. Make sure that it's at least 73 percent sodium chlorite with no other chemicals or harmful additives.

Iodine

Remember the red disinfectant from your childhood that goes on cuts and scrapes and burns like crazy? It's also good for purifying water. It changes the taste and color of your water, but either liquid 2 percent iodine tincture or commercially available iodine tablets will work. Iodine isn't completely effective when it comes to killing harmful protozoa that can make you sick, but if you add 8 drops of liquid iodine to a gallon of clear water or 16 drops per gallon of cloudy water, it will kill most bacteria and viruses.

Water Purification Tablets (Chlorine Dioxide)

These are perhaps the easiest way to kill everything in water that could harm you, especially if you have to leave your home, but they take about four hours to work. They don't expire and they don't change the taste or color of your water, so they are great options whether you're in your home or have to leave in a hurry. Make them part of your emergency supply and add some to your bug-out bag as well.

UV Light Purification

Several different types of ultraviolet light machines are used to purify water, but to be truthful, they are much less effective than heat or chemical purification methods. The water has to be clear, and UV light doesn't kill viruses. Considering how easy the other more effective methods are, this just isn't the way to go as far as most preppers are concerned.

As you can see, there are many different options at your disposal when you're making plans to meet your water purification needs. Which one you choose is entirely up to you, and you should base your decision on what type of disaster you're planning for and what your individual water needs are. The most important thing is that you do prepare, because without water, you won't make it for long.

SECTION 2
Water-Bath and Pressure Canning

- **Chapter 4:** Water-Bath versus Pressure Canning

- **Chapter 5:** Getting Started with Water-Bath Canning

- **Chapter 6:** Preserving Jellies, Jams, and Other Sweet Spreads

- **Chapter 7:** Canning Fruit

- **Chapter 8:** Pickling

- **Chapter 9:** Salsas and Relishes

- **Chapter 10:** Getting Started with Pressure Canning

- **Chapter 11:** Pressure Canning Recipes

4

WATER-BATH VERSUS PRESSURE CANNING

Learning to preserve food via canning is a great way to efficiently stock many different types of food for both daily use and emergency preparedness at a minimal cost. Another benefit is that you know exactly what goes into your jars; you don't have to worry about hidden chemicals or loads of sodium.

Canning a variety of foods allows you to eat whatever you want at whatever time of year you like, and it will be just as delicious as when it was harvested. Remember that fresh fruits and vegetables from your own garden or from a farmers' market are the best choices for canning. When done correctly, canning also preserves most of the nutrients in your foods, so in an emergency situation, you'll still be well fed and you won't need to worry about food fatigue.

Nearly anything you like can be made and canned, ranging from simple meals to delicious side dishes, condiments, and even complex desserts. Basically, what you preserve through canning is limited only by your imagination and a few basic rules.

Avoiding Botulism

For canning, foods are divided into two groups according to pH levels: strong-acid foods and strong-alkali (low-acid) foods. To prevent the growth of *Clostridium botulinum,* the microorganism that causes botulism, each group has its own method of canning.

Strong-acid foods can be canned using the water-bath, or boiling water, method of canning because their higher acid levels prevent the growth of the organism. Strong-alkali foods must be pressure canned because they require higher temperatures for longer periods of time to kill and inhibit the growth of *C. botulinum.*

Fruits, jams, jellies, fruit juices, pickles, tomatoes, relishes, condiments, salsas, and chutneys are all examples of strong-acid foods. See the chart below for the pH rating of some popular canning foods. High-acid foods are fairly easy to preserve and provide a whole new level of flavor to your cooking.

STRONG ACID				STRONG ALKALI		
1	2	3	4	5	6	7
	citrus		apples	carrots		corn
		apricots			asparagus	peas
	pickles		tomatoes	green beans		chicken
		blackberries		beets		shrimp
	gooseberries				fish	
		peaches				ham
	plums	pears		ground beef		
		strawberries			potatoes	dairy products
Use water-bath canning method				Use pressure-canning method		

Vegetables, meats, and some sauces are examples of low-acid foods that need to be preserved using the pressure-canning method to destroy and prevent the growth of *C. botulinum* spores and other harmful organisms. This is a bit more complicated at first and requires special equipment, but pressure canning is a piece of cake once you get the hang of it.

Since strong-acid foods require the simpler method of canning (water bath), they tend to be more popular among beginners.

Water-Bath Canning

Water-bath canning is a relatively simple process that involves packing your food into jars and boiling them to increase the temperature inside the jars enough to kill residual bacteria and force air out of the jars so they seal. The environment inside the jars will then prohibit the growth of organisms that cause spoilage and disease.

All that you need besides jars, lids, and bands is a stockpot deep enough to submerge the jars in boiling water and racks in which to place the jars. Water-bath canners with jar racks that fit perfectly into the canner are readily available, relatively inexpensive, and preferred. This method is perfectly acceptable for use with high-acid foods that have a pH lower than 4.6, such as fruits and some vegetables. Tomatoes are typically canned as a high-acid food, but you should probably add a bit of vinegar, lemon juice, or citric acid to increase the acidity enough to create an environment prohibitive to *C. botulinum*.

With water-bath canning, racks are placed in stockpots or water-bath canners filled with water, and the pot is brought to a boil on a stove top. The filled canning jars are placed on these racks and processed (boiled) for specific times according to the food being canned. Then the jars are cooled, which is when the lids seal shut. Once the jars have cooled and the seals are tightly shut, bands are added to the jars and the food can be stored away.

Pressure Canning

As the name implies, this method of canning uses a pressurized canner to increase the heat inside the jars enough to kill *C. botulinum* in low-acid foods. This method has a dangerous element to it because you are dealing with a highly pressurized metal container full of hot water, food, and glass, so you need to exercise caution. That being said, it's a perfectly safe process as long as you follow safety procedures, and it is an excellent way to preserve foods such as meats and vegetables.

Both types of pressure canning use a pot with a lid that typically has a rubber seal that swells and keeps the pressure inside the pot. The lid will have a steam vent or petcock in the top, which is a short, hollow pipe that goes from the inside to the outside and vents the pressure canner when it's open or holds the steam in when it's closed. This is what the gauge attaches to in order to regulate the pressure. Don't ever remove this when the pot is pressurized. Pressure canners come in many sizes, and which one you choose will depend primarily on how many jars you want to process at one time. As in water-bath canning, metal racks are placed in the pressure canner, the canner is filled with water, and the jars are placed inside. The jars are processed under pressure (dictated by the foods you're canning) for a certain period of time (also dictated by the foods you're canning) and then removed to cool and seal.

Weighted Gauges Versus Dial Gauges

There are two types of pressure canners: ones that use a weighted gauge and ones that use a dial gauge. A dial gauge actually has a pressure gauge on top that you set to the desired pressure and trust that it's accurate. If you choose to use a gauge canner, you should calibrate your gauges at least once per year to ensure that they're accurate. Even a few degrees can be the difference between safe-to-eat and botulism or other foodborne illnesses.

Another downside of dial gauges is the cost. Whereas you can pick up a weighted-gauge pressure canner for a few bucks at a thrift store, dial-gauge pressure canners are going to cost you significantly more. Also, dial-gauge canners simply have more moving parts that can break or cause inaccuracy.

Weighted-gauge pressure canners simply rely on a weighted piece of metal that's simple, easy, accurate, and durable. It really is just a matter of personal preference, so whichever you're more comfortable with, go for it. It should be noted that you can't adjust the dial gauge to allow for altitude, so if you're at a higher altitude you may be better off using a weighted-gauge canner.

Remember that regardless of which method you use, you're dealing with extremely hot glass that, although tempered to be more tolerant to temperatures, will shatter with extreme changes from hot to cold or vice versa. Keep fans and drafts off your jars as you're taking them from the pot and be gentle with them. Even tapping a hot jar on the edge of the counter can shatter it.

Whichever method you choose to learn first, you may want to borrow the equipment and purchase only a few jars to limit your investment until you know for certain that canning is for you. Start out with very simple foods and recipes, such as dill pickles, tomato sauce, or canned peaches, and gradually work your way toward more complex recipes and even trying your own variations. When you're completely comfortable with both the science and the process of your first method of canning, then you can confidently start learning the other.

Since water-bath canning is more popular and requires less specialized equipment, it's a great place for beginning canners to start, so we'll do the same.

5

GETTING STARTED WITH
WATER-BATH CANNING

To be well organized and prepared to water-bath can, it's best to gather your supplies and get them ready before you gather your ingredients. Having all of your tools and ingredients readily available will make the process go more smoothly.

Although you can buy used canning jars and bands or reuse yours for many years, you do need to make sure they're in good condition. Jars that have chips or bands that are bent may hinder the sealing and are more likely to break when heated. However, you cannot reuse lids. Once you break the seal to open your jars, the lids are most likely warped and unable to reseal. So instead of running the risk of wasting your food, toss all used lids and buy new ones.

You may hear of people canning with recycled glass jars (from commercially packaged mayonnaise, applesauce, or other products). This is not recommended. These jars may not be made of glass that can withstand the high temperatures of canning, and lids and bands may not fit tightly enough on recycled jars. In any case, used canning jars can be had for pennies, so the cost savings just isn't worth the risk. The following checklist will help you get organized.

Prepper's Checklist — Water-Bath Canning

- ☐ Large water-bath canner
- ☐ One or more canning racks
- ☐ Thermometer for testing food and water temperatures
- ☐ Jar lifter (tongs used to lift hot jars from the canner)
- ☐ Jars (½ pint, pint, or quart sizes)
- ☐ Canning funnel
- ☐ New lids for each jar
- ☐ Bands for each jar
- ☐ Clean dish towels for wiping jar rims
- ☐ Clean dish towels for cooling the hot jars
- ☐ Butter knife or thin spatula for removing air bubbles
- ☐ Watch or kitchen timer
- ☐ Marker and labels

Basic Instructions for Water-Bath Canning

Being prepared will make the process much easier, especially until you form your own routine. Once you have it down, it will be just like anything else; you'll develop a rhythm and preferences. Until you find your rhythm, follow these foolproof steps and you'll have a pantry full of delicious, nutritious food in no time!

1. Wash all of your jars, lids, and bands in hot, soapy water. Make sure to rinse them well and allow them to air-dry.

2. When working with glass, you want to minimize the risk of breakage. The best way to do this is to simmer, not boil, your jars in the canner as you're preparing the food, and at the same time, simmer the lids and bands in a saucepan of water to keep them warm until you are ready to pour the ingredients into them.

3. If the jars are too cool when the ingredients are added to them, they're more likely to crack or break from the sudden temperature change. If you have a dishwasher this step can be simplified. You can easily load your dishwasher with the bands and jars and wash and heat them that way. Leave them in the closed dishwasher until ready to fill.

4. After everything is washed, prepare the canner. If you don't already have one, that's fine. Simply find a pot in your kitchen that is large enough to allow the jars to be completely submerged in the water with about 1 to 2 inches above the lids. It must have a lid and a rack.

5. Next you need to prepare all of your ingredients for the recipe and read your instructions well. Always read them twice so there's less chance of error.

6. Put your lids and bands in a saucepan of hot water so that the sealing compound will be soft and ready to seal to the top of your jar.

7. Close any windows and turn off any fans that will direct airflow on or toward your hot, filled jars, because the change in temperature can cause the jars to explode, especially right after processing.

8. When you're ready to put your ingredients in a jar, remove the jar from the hot water using jar tongs. Be sure to fill jars one at a time; using a funnel makes this task easier and safer and will also help keep the rims of the jars clean so that the seal will form. Some recipes call for a specific headspace (space left empty at the top of the jar). This space is generally ¼ inch for jellies, jams, and juices, and ½ inch for whole fruits, pickles, tomatoes, and salsas.

9. It's always a good idea to remove the air bubbles from the jar even if the directions don't specifically say to. You can buy a gadget made just for this or simply work a butter knife or rubber spatula back and forth in the jar to release any bubbles.

10. Always use a damp kitchen towel or paper towel to rid the rim and threads of any food residue that may have leaked out while filling. Residue on the rims or seal can cause dangerous spoilage.

11. Remove the lids from the hot water and place onto the jars. Make sure the lids are centered correctly. The seal must be lined up with the threads of the jar. Secure the band until fingertip tight, but no tighter. Remember, the idea is for air to escape from the jar during the boiling process in order to form the seal and prevent spoilage.

12. Place the filled jars onto the rack and lower it into the canner. Make sure that the water is 1 to 2 inches above the jars, to allow boiling over the jar. This makes sure everything in the jar gets preserved properly.

13. Put the lid on the canner and follow the processing instructions in the recipe. In most cases, you'll turn the heat on the stove top to high, place the lid on the canner, and bring to a vigorous boil.

14. Once the water is boiling vigorously, start the kitchen timer for the required processing time. Processing time always starts from the boiling point. Be sure to take into consideration your altitude if you are at a higher altitude. See the next page for an altitude chart. You'll also find an altitude chart for selected cities in the United States and Canada at the back of the book.

15. When the timer goes off, turn off the burner and remove the lid of the canner. Allow the jars to rest in the water for at least five minutes; this allows the temperature of the jars to gradually adjust to the outside temperature. This is important to reduce risk of cracking, but remember that the food in the jars continues to cook as long as the jars are in the hot water.

Altitude in Feet	Altitude in Meters	Additional Processing Time
1,000 – 3,000	305 – 914	5 Minutes
3,001 – 6,000	915 – 1,829	10 Minutes
6,001 – 8,000	1,830 – 2,438	15 Minutes
8,001 – 10,000	2,439 – 3,048	20 Minutes

16. After the jars have cooled for at least five minutes, carefully remove them. Place them upright onto a thick-folded towel; this prevents temperature shock between the jar and the surface area, which can cause the glass to break.

17. Do not touch the jars for a minimum of twelve to twenty-four hours.

18. Don't panic if your seal has not sealed within twenty-four hours; the food can be reprocessed or you can put it in the fridge and use it first.

19. Now the only thing left to do is to label each jar lid and store in a dark, cool, dry place.

Checking for a Seal

There are three ways to check for a proper seal:

- The best way to check for a good seal is to push down on the center of the lid. If there is no give, then the seal is good.

- You can also tap the center of the lid with a spoon. If it makes a high-pitched ring, it's sealed, but if it makes a dull thud, it isn't.

- Finally, you can hold the jar at eye level and look straight across the lid. The lid should be slightly concave (curved down in the center). If the center of the lid is either slightly bulging or is flat, it may not be sealed.

If you find any jars that don't have a tight seal, then simply put those jars in the fridge and eat the contents within five days, or repeat the canning process immediately.

Tips for Water-Bath Canning Safety and Food Handling

- Always check the recipe, your manufacturer's guide, or your local agricultural extension office to be sure that the type of food you're canning has enough acidity to be canned in a water-bath canner.

- If you're canning mixed foods containing both high- and low-acid foods (e.g., some soups, relishes, stews), they must be processed in a pressure canner to ensure against bacterial growth and spoilage.

- Always wipe the rims of the jars with a clean towel before placing the lids on the jars. Food and liquids on the rims of the jars can prevent them from sealing properly.

- When selecting and preparing foods for canning, always check carefully for mold, bruises, holes, and cuts that may harbor bacteria or insect eggs.

- If there are children present, be sure they're safely away from the stove and the canner during processing and that they understand that jostling or moving the jars during cooling can interfere with proper (and safe) sealing.

- Always make sure that your cooling jars are safe from jostling or tipping for at least 12 to 24 hours. You may want to keep pets and small children out of the kitchen during the cooling period.

As you can see, water-bath canning is a fairly simple process, and the extra tips and hints included in this book will make canning all of your favorite foods even easier. Before getting to the recipes, the next chapter addresses a few additional tips about one of the most popular canning groups: sweet spreads.

6

PRESERVING JELLIES, JAMS, AND OTHER SWEET SPREADS

Jams and jellies are versatile and can be used for just about anything in the kitchen. Preserving your own jellies and jams is a great way to have wonderful summer flavors all year round, waste less produce, and save a lot of money on store-bought spreads. Also, many store brands contain unwanted ingredients and tons of sugar. There's no reason to pay more when you can make your own at home and decide exactly what goes in it and what stays out.

Jelly and jam have several different textures, flavors, colors, and uses. Most people only think of jelly or jam for breakfast. However, there are thousands of different possibilities when creating your own. For example, jalapeño jam is a great way to spice up a meal.

There are several different types of spreads. Here are the most common:

- **Jelly** is a semisolid mix of juice and sugar that's firm enough to hold its shape.

- **Jam** is a jelly that contains bits of crushed fruit or vegetable.

- **Preserves** are small fruits left whole or fruit cut into pieces and preserved in thick, clear, jellied syrup.

- **Marmalades** have more concentrated flavors and are soft jellies often containing only the peel of citrus fruits.

- **Compotes** are made with either whole pieces or large chunks of fresh or dried fruits that have been simmered down in a syrup made from sugar and possibly other seasonings.

- **Chutneys** are thick sauces made from fruits, spices, sugar, and vinegar. The fruit is generally pureed or cooked down to make part of the sauce, and there may or may not be chunks.

Pectin

Sweet spreads consist of preserved fruits using sugar and sometimes a thickening ingredient called *pectin*. Pectin is a substance that can turn into a jelly texture when matched with the correct amount of acid and sugar. It can be found in all fruits, but some contain more than others. You can buy pectin at most grocery stores in the baking aisle, or you can blend fruits with low pectin amounts with other fruits that contain a higher amount of pectin.

For example, cranberries contain a ton of pectin and therefore no added pectin is required to create a spread. So if you want to make berry jam, you can add cranberries to it to raise the pectin levels. Cranberries are also a great way to cut down the sweetness level of a spread that may have extra-sweet berries in it, such as strawberries.

Prep Tip   Powdered pectin won't dissolve in a high-sugar mix, so dissolve it with the fruit prior to adding sugar. If you're using liquid pectin, add it after the sugar. Use pectin within a year of purchase for best results.

Here are some useful tips for making your jams, jellies, and preserves delicious and successful:

Tips for Making Jams, Jellies, and Preserves

- Making these in small batches helps ensure that the fruit will cook quickly and the color and flavor will be better.

- When you're creating your own jam and jelly recipes, remember this guideline: for every cup of fruit you use, you'll want to add ¾ cup of sugar. For example, 4 cups of fruit will require 3 cups of sugar. Some low-sugar recipes and recipes using apples and other high-pectin fruits can use less, but this is a good general rule.

- Something to keep in mind when choosing your fruits is that perfectly ripe fruit or really sweet fruits contain less pectin than barely ripe fruits. So when picking or purchasing, choose slightly unripe fruit for your spreads.

- If you are using very ripe or especially sweet fruit, add 1 to 2 tablespoons of fresh or bottled lemon juice. The acid in the lemon juice will help the mixture thicken.

- You do need to watch out for scorching or burning fruit, as the sugar in the recipe can burn quickly. The best ways to prevent this are to watch your heat and adjust to a lower setting if needed, and to stir almost constantly during the cooking process.

- To test your jam or preserves to see if they're done, take a spoonful out of the pan and set it aside. If it holds its shape after about a minute, you should be ready to start canning the mixture.

- Always be sure to adjust times based on altitude.

The Science of Gelling

Jelly and jam making is, to a certain degree, an original exercise in molecular gastronomy. To turn fruit and syrup into a delicious spread, you must have the perfect ratio of sugar to pectin to acid, and then cook it to the gelling point for your elevation. Pectin is a polysaccharide found in fruit, but it's negatively charged, which means that its individual ions naturally move away from each other.

Acid, also found naturally in fruits, changes the charge to a more neutral state, allowing the molecules to move closer together. This is why it's important to add lemon juice or citric acid to low-acid fruits when you're making jellies.

The third necessary component of gelling, sugar, enters the scene at this point. Even with the higher acid content neutralizing the pectin, there's still too much water for the pectin to bind into a firm gel. When heated, the sugar binds the water, which brings the pectin molecules together and forms a gel.

Natural Additives and Preservatives Used for Jams and Jellies

- **Salt**—added for flavor; is only a preservative when used in large quantities such as during brining

- **Sugar, honey, corn syrup**—preserves texture, color, and integrity of fruit; assists in gelling

- **Vinegar**—increases acidity to help fight botulism and increase shelf life (i.e., pickling)

- **Artificial sweeteners**—used to flavor water; do *not* use as a replacement for sugar

- **Pectin**—used to guarantee thickening of jellies because fresh fruit often has low pectin levels

- **Citric acid**—increases acidity of jellies so that they gel

- **Lemon juice or vitamin C (ascorbic acid)**—combats the enzymatic reaction between air and cut fruit that causes the fruit to turn brown. Dissolve 1 teaspoon of ascorbic acid or lemon juice in 1 gallon of water, and then soak your fruit in it.

Making Sure Your Jelly Gels

Nothing is more frustrating to beginning canners than making your jelly, processing it, and waiting for it to set just to find out that it's too runny. This happens when the acid-to-sugar-to-pectin ratio is off and can generally be avoided by using commercial powdered or liquid pectin. But what if you don't have any or don't want to use it? That's okay, too. You can do a few things to increase your chances for success:

- Use slightly underripe fruit because it will have more pectin.

- Add a few drops of ascorbic acid if you're using really ripe fruit.

- Use a candy thermometer to make sure that you cook your jelly to 220 degrees F. That's the gelling point for sugar mixtures at sea level. If you're in higher elevations, add 2 degrees for every 1,000 feet above sea level that you are at.

Testing for Doneness

It's a ton easier to fix your jelly-that-isn't-jelly before it's out of the pot than after you've already wasted time and energy processing it. Besides the temperature test, there are a couple of other ways to determine whether or not your product has gelled sufficiently to jar.

- **Refrigerator test**—Dribble a drop or two of jelly onto a chilled plate and place it in the fridge for a few minutes. If it gels, it's done.

- **Spoon test**—Dip a chilled spoon into the jelly. If the product drips right off of the spoon in separate droplets, it's not done. If it "sheets" together off of the spoon instead of in separate drops, it's done.

The following are several fairly simple recipes for a variety of spreads and other delicious recipes that you can make using the water-bath method of canning for preservation. If you opt to use vegetables instead of fruits, you may need to add a few drops of ascorbic acid or lemon juice to increase the acidity to safe levels. Follow all instructions for jar and seal preparation discussed earlier to set the scene for canning success!

Classic Grape Jelly

Grape jelly is a great place to start your canning experience. It's a kid favorite, and it's easy to make once you get the hang of it. You can make just about any flavor jelly using this recipe. Simply substitute the grape juice with the juice of your choice.

- 3 cups unsweetened grape juice
- 1 (2-ounce) package powdered fruit pectin
- 5¼ cups granulated sugar
- 3 pint jars, lids, and bands

1. Fill the canner with enough water to cover the jars. Boil the water, reduce the heat to low, place the jars in the water, and simmer until ready to use. Prepare lids and bands by simmering them over low heat in a small saucepan.

2. In a large saucepan combine the pectin and grape juice over medium-high heat. Bring the mixture to a boil and stir for about a minute.

3. Stir in the sugar until completely dissolved. Remove the pot from the heat and skim off any foam.

4. Quickly pour the hot jelly mixture into the jars, leaving ½ inch of headspace.

5. Remove air bubbles, wipe rims, center the lids, and screw on the bands and adjust until they are fingertip tight.

6. Place the jars in the canner and bring to a boil. Make sure there is at least 1 inch of water covering the jars.

7. Process for 10 minutes, adjusting for altitude. Remove the jars from the canner and cool.

Spicy Jalapeño Jelly

This jelly covers all the bases with its mix of sweet and spicy flavors. This is a great gift for anyone with a taste for fiery foods, and it tastes great on crackers or even in a sandwich.

- 16 jalapeño peppers, divided
- 1 large green bell pepper
- 1½ cups apple cider vinegar
- 4¼ cups granulated sugar
- Pinch of salt
- 4 ounces liquid pectin
- 2 half-pint jars, lids, and bands

1. Fill the canner with enough water to cover the jars. Boil the water, reduce the heat to low, place the jars in the water, and simmer until ready to use. Prepare lids and bands by simmering them over low heat in a small saucepan.

2. Seed and finely chop 4 of the jalapeño peppers, and set aside.

3. Combine the green bell pepper and the remaining whole jalapeño peppers in a food processor or blender. Process until nicely minced and smooth. This may need to be done in more than one batch to fit into the blender or food processor.

4. Pour the pepper mix into a large saucepan, and mix in the apple cider vinegar.

5. Bring to a boil and let simmer for 15 to 20 minutes. Strain the mixture through at least two layers of cheesecloth. If you do not have any cheesecloth, a large spoon and a fine mesh strainer will work as well. You should have about 1 cup of liquid.

6. Pour the fine mixture back into the saucepan, and stir in the sugar and salt until well blended.

7. Bring to a boil over medium-high heat. When the mix comes to a rolling boil, continue to boil for 1 minute, and then add in the liquid pectin.

8. Add the finely chopped jalapeño peppers, and ladle the mixture into sterile jars, leaving ¼ inch of headspace.

9. Remove air bubbles, wipe rims, center the lids, and screw on the bands and adjust until they are fingertip tight.

10. Place the jars in the canner and bring to a boil. Make sure there is at least 1 inch of water covering the jars.

11. Process for 10 minutes, adjusting for altitude. Remove the jars from the canner and cool.

Herb Jelly

This recipe is great for making savory sweet jellies that go nicely with dinner breads. Feel free to mix and match the herbs and add more or less to suit your taste.

- 1¼ cups boiling water
- 2 tablespoons minced fresh rosemary, basil, thyme, or other herbs
- 3 cups granulated sugar
- ¼ cup white vinegar
- 1 (3-ounce) pouch liquid fruit pectin
- 2 drops green food coloring (if desired)
- 4 half-pint jars, lids, and bands

1. Fill the canner with enough water to cover the jars. Boil the water, reduce the heat to low, place the jars in the water, and simmer until ready to use. Prepare lids and bands by simmering them over low heat in a small saucepan.

2. In a large saucepan, combine the boiling water and herbs. Cover and let sit for approximately 15 minutes. You may strain the herbs out or leave them in—it's entirely up to you. If the liquid does not yield 1¼ cups, add water until it does.

3. Add the sugar and vinegar. Bring to a full rolling boil over high heat, stirring constantly.

4. Add the pectin. Boil hard and stir for 1 minute.

5. Take the saucepan off the heat and remove any foam. Add food coloring if desired.

6. Pour the hot mixture into jars, leaving ¼ inch of headspace.

7. Remove air bubbles, wipe rims, center the lids, and screw on the bands and adjust until they are fingertip tight.

8. Place the jars in the canner and bring to a boil. Make sure there is at least 1 inch of water covering the jars.

9. Process for 10 minutes, adjusting for altitude. Remove the jars from the canner and cool.

Any-Fruit Jam

As the title says, you can use just about any fruit for this simple jam recipe, although you may have to experiment a bit with the pectin and sugar to get the equation just right. For the best flavor possible, it's best to have a mix of semi-ripe and ripe fruit on hand.

- 4½ cups pitted, chopped fruit of your choice
- ½ cup water
- 7½ cups granulated sugar
- 1 (1¾-ounce) package powdered fruit pectin
- 8 half-pint canning jars with lids and bands

1. Fill the canner with enough water to cover the jars. Boil the water, reduce the heat to low, place the jars in the water, and simmer until ready to use. Prepare lids and bands by simmering them over low heat in a small saucepan.

2. Place the fruit and water into a large saucepan and bring to a boil.

3. Reduce the heat to medium-low, cover, and simmer for about 5 minutes. Stir in the sugar, and remove the foam if necessary.

4. Bring the mixture to a full boil over high heat, stirring constantly, and then mix in the pectin. Return the mixture to a full boil, and boil for 1 minute, stirring constantly. Remove from the heat, and skim off any foam.

5. Pour the hot mixture into jars, leaving ¼ inch of headspace.

6. Remove air bubbles, wipe rims, center the lids, and screw on the bands and adjust until they are fingertip tight.

7. Place the jars in the canner and bring to a boil. Make sure there is at least 1 inch of water covering the jars.

8. Process for 10 minutes, adjusting for altitude. Remove the jars from the canner and cool.

Nutty Pecan Jam

In a survival situation, you want a source of protein, carbs, and fat. This is a delicious combination of all three and will liven up the flavor of stale bread or whatever else you may choose to eat it on.

- 1 cup chopped pecans
- 1 cup granulated sugar
- ¼ cup unsalted butter
- 1 tablespoon brown sugar
- 1 tablespoon ground ginger
- 1 tablespoon ground cinnamon
- 1 tablespoon apple cider vinegar
- Pinch of salt
- 2 half-pint jars, lids, and bands

1. Fill the canner with enough water to cover the jars. Boil the water, reduce the heat to low, place the jars in the water, and simmer until ready to use. Prepare lids and bands by simmering them over low heat in a small saucepan.

2. In a large saucepan, combine all of the ingredients.

3. Cook over medium heat, until the sugar has dissolved and the mixture is blended. Do not let the mixture boil, or you'll end up with pecan candy or worse yet, a gritty mess.

4. Pour the hot mixture into jars, leaving ¼ inch of headspace.

5. Remove air bubbles, wipe rims, center the lids, and screw on the bands and adjust until they are fingertip tight.

6. Place the jars in the canner and bring to a boil. Make sure there is at least 1 inch of water covering the jars.

7. Process for 10 minutes, adjusting for altitude. Remove the jars from the canner and cool.

7

CANNING FRUIT

Canning fruit is very easy and a great way for beginners to pick up canning. Since fruit is a high-acid food, the water-bath canning method is the only method you need to use.

When choosing fruit, it is best to use them in the peak of their seasons. Also important, fruit for canning needs to be picked just before they are truly ripe. That way, the canning process brings out all the flavors of that fruit and the fruit will hold their shape well.

Hot Pack Versus Cold Pack

There are two different ways to can your fresh fruit, or even your pickles or fresh vegetables: by hot packing them or by cold packing them. Hot packing involves heating or cooking the produce with the liquid and packing it all together into the jars for processing. Cold packing involves packing the raw produce tightly into the jars and then pouring the boiling liquid over them prior to processing. Between the two, hot packing creates richer, more blended flavors.

Hot packing is best for nice, firm fruits that won't get mushy if you heat them, like blueberries, or if you're making such mixes as apple pie filling. Cold packing (also known as raw packing) allows you to can soft produce like raspberries or peaches without ending up with preserves. Cold packing can be used for just about any fruit, but hot packing is good if you'd like them to cook a bit first. Directions for both methods follow.

Hot Pack

1. Measure out the fruit and gather your ingredients. Place the fruit in a large saucepan with the correct amount of sugar and any other spices that you're using.

2. Set the saucepan aside and let the fruit mixture marinate for about 2 hours.

3. Then heat the fruit mixture until the juices are flowing out of the fruit and everything is warm, similar to compote.

4. Fill the canning jars, leaving ½ inch of headspace. If you run out of liquid, add boiling water until all jars are full enough. Remove air bubbles and wipe the rims clean.

5. Secure the lids and bands, and process using the water-bath method. Don't forget to let the jars cool, and don't mess with the lids while the jars are cooling. Also, adjust cooking times to your altitude as needed.

Cold Pack

1. First, make your syrup based on the following ratios:

    - Very light (sugar water)—½ cup sugar to 5 cups water
    - Light—1 cup sugar to 5 cups water
    - Medium—1½ cups sugar to 5 cups water
    - Heavy—2 cups sugar to 5 cups water
    - Very heavy—2½ cups sugar to 5 cups water

    This is a great way to adjust the sugar depending on what you're canning or what you plan to use the syrup for. For instance, pie fillings will be thick, but canned fruits made to eat straight out of the jar are delicious with just a light syrup. For that matter, if you don't want to add any sweetness, feel free to use only water and let the natural sugars of the fruit sweeten it. Regardless of which syrup you're using, follow these steps to can your produce:

2. Peel, core, and clean your produce. Remove any damaged spots, and slice as necessary.

3. Heat the sugar and water in a saucepan over medium-high heat until the sugar is completely dissolved.

4. Pour about ½ cup of liquid into each jar. Pack the produce gently into the jar about halfway up. Then gently tap the bottom of the glass on a pot holder or towel on your counter. This helps settle the produce and release bubbles without having to smash delicate berries or fruits into the jar.

5. Fill the jars until full, tapping when necessary to pack tightly. No matter how tightly they seem to be packed, as soon as you add the liquid, space is going to appear.

6. Cover with liquid until ½ inch of headspace is left.

7. Remove air bubbles, wipe rims, center the lids, and screw on the bands and adjust until they are fingertip tight.

8. Process in the canner for 10 minutes (or for the time each recipe states), adjusting for altitude.

9. Remove the jars and set upright on a towel. Do not disturb jars for at least 24 hours.

Canned Peaches

- 9 pounds of peaches (3 pounds per quart)
- 4 cups water
- 2 cups granulated sugar
- 3 quart jars, lids, and bands

1. Fill the canner with enough water to cover the jars. Boil the water, reduce the heat to low, place the jars in the water, and simmer until ready to use. Prepare lids and bands by simmering them over low heat in a small saucepan.

2. Fill a large pot with water and bring to a boil. Add the peaches to the boiling water and boil for 30 seconds. Plunge into a large bowl of icy cold water to loosen the skins. Slip off the skins, then cut the peaches in half and remove the pits.

3. Pack the peaches into the jars, leaving ½ inch of headspace.

4. In a saucepan, mix the water and sugar and bring to a boil, stirring to dissolve the sugar. Pour enough syrup over the peaches to cover, leaving ½ inch of headspace.

5. Remove air bubbles, wipe rims, center the lids, and screw on the bands and adjust until they are fingertip tight.

6. Place the jars in the canner and bring to a boil. Make sure there is at least 1 inch of water covering the jars.

7. Process for 25–30 minutes, adjusting for altitude. Remove the jars from the canner and cool.

Apple Pie Filling

- 6–7 quarts apples, peeled, cored, and quartered
- 4½ cups granulated sugar
- 1 cup cornstarch
- 3 teaspoons ground cinnamon
- ¼ teaspoon ground nutmeg
- ¼ teaspoon ground ginger
- 1 teaspoon salt
- 10 cups water
- 5 tablespoons fresh or bottled lemon juice, divided
- 6–7 quart jars, lids, and bands

1. Fill the canner with enough water to cover the jars. Boil the water, reduce the heat to low, place the jars in the water, and simmer until ready to use. Prepare lids and bands by simmering them over low heat in a small saucepan.

2. To keep the apples from turning brown, place them in a large bowl with cold water and 2 tablespoons lemon juice.

3. Mix the dry ingredients together in a large pot. Add the water and cook the mixture until thick. Add the remaining lemon juice.

4. Pack the apples into the jars, and pour the cooked filling over the apples, leaving ½ inch of headspace.

5. Remove air bubbles, wipe rims, center the lids, and screw on the bands and adjust until they are fingertip tight.

6. Place the jars in the canner and bring to a boil. Make sure there is at least 1 inch of water covering the jars.

7. Process for 20 minutes, adjusting for altitude. Remove the jars from the canner and cool.

Blueberry Compote

- 4 cups granulated sugar
- 2 cups water
- 8 cups fresh blueberries
- ⅓ cup fresh or bottled lemon juice
- 3 pint jars, lids, and bands

1. Fill the canner with enough water to cover the jars. Boil the water, reduce the heat to low, place the jars in the water, and simmer until ready to use. Prepare lids and bands by simmering them over low heat in a small saucepan.

2. Combine the sugar and water in a saucepan, and boil for 5 minutes. Add the blueberries, and simmer for another 4 to 5 minutes or until the blueberries start to break down and burst open.

3. Remove from the heat and stir in the lemon juice.

4. Fill the jars with the blueberry mixture, leaving ¼ to ½ inch of headspace.

5. Remove air bubbles, wipe rims, center the lids, and screw on the bands and adjust until they are fingertip tight.

6. Place the jars in the canner and bring to a boil. Make sure there is at least 1 inch of water covering the jars.

7. Process for 10 minutes, adjusting for altitude. Remove the jars from the canner and cool.

8

PICKLING

Pickling is a great way to preserve fruits and vegetables, and although you usually think of cucumbers, you can pickle just about anything! Pickled eggs, pickled watermelon rind, and pickled jalapeños are just a few examples of noncucumber produce that is canned regularly.

Types of Pickling

Although all forms of pickling involve the use of some type of acid (typically vinegar) to increase the pH (thus making it *Clostridium botulinum*–resistant), there are four different methods that you can use.

Brining

Likely the most traditional form of pickling, brining has been used for centuries to make cucumber pickles, sauerkraut, and other foods. In this process, the produce is fermented in salt and water for at least a week, and sometimes for months. The process makes the produce tender yet firm, and the salt used in brining acts as a preservative. Brining can be done with any type of container, but it needs to be stored in a cool, dry place while the process occurs.

Fresh-Pack Pickling

Also called quick-process pickling, this process involves short-term brining for just a few hours or possibly overnight. The brining is actually more of a process to help preserve and maintain the structure and texture of the produce. After the brining, the produce is stuffed into jars and the hot pickling liquid is poured over them prior to processing.

Relishes

Relishes are fruits or vegetables that are chopped up and cooked in a vinegar pickling solution. Common relishes are sweet or dill pickle relish, mango relish, and pepper relishes.

Fruit Pickles

It may sound odd, but fruit pickles are actually quite delicious. They're made from whole or sliced fruits and even rinds that are combined with a sweet and spicy syrup that has lemon juice or vinegar. You can also use some of your favorite spices if you'd like, as well.

Classic Dill Pickle Spears

- 11 cups water
- 5 cups white vinegar
- 1 cup pickling salt
- 12 pounds pickling cucumbers, cut into spears
- 9 fresh dill sprigs or heads
- 18 whole cloves garlic
- 18 dried hot chilies
- 9 quart jars, lids, and bands

1. Fill the canner with enough water to cover the jars. Boil the water, reduce the heat to low, place the jars in the water, and simmer until ready to use. Prepare lids and bands by simmering them over low heat in a small saucepan.

2. In a large pot, bring the water, vinegar, and salt to a boil. Boil for 10 minutes.

3. Place the cucumbers into the jars, leaving ½ inch of headspace.

4. Add 1 dill head or sprig, two garlic cloves, and two chilies into each jar.

5. Carefully ladle the hot mixture into the jars, leaving ½ inch of headspace.

6. Remove air bubbles, wipe rims, center the lids, and screw on the bands and adjust until they are fingertip tight.

7. Place the jars in the canner and bring to a boil. Make sure there is at least 1 inch of water covering the jars.

8. Process for 15 minutes, adjusting for altitude. Remove the jars from the canner and cool.

Pickled Beets

- 10 pounds beets
- 5 cups white vinegar
- 2½ cups granulated sugar
- 1 tablespoon pickling salt
- 5 tablespoons whole cloves
- 5 quart jars, lids, and bands

1. Fill the canner with enough water to cover the jars. Boil the water, reduce the heat to low, place the jars in the water, and simmer until ready to use. Prepare lids and bands by simmering them over low heat in a small saucepan.

2. Place the beets in a large stockpot and cover with water. Bring to a boil and cook until tender, about 15 minutes. Remove from the heat and cool. Peel the beets, and if the beets are large, slice or quarter them. (Small beets can remain whole.)

3. Place all of the ingredients except the beets and cloves in a nonreactive saucepan. Over high heat, bring to a rolling boil and then remove from the heat.

4. Stuff the beets into the jars as tightly as possible without smashing them, leaving 1 inch of headspace. Pour the brine into the jar, leaving 1 inch of headspace. Add a clove to each jar.

5. Remove air bubbles, wipe rims, center the lids, and screw on the bands and adjust until they are fingertip tight.

6. Place the jars in the canner and bring to a boil. Make sure there is at least 1 inch of water covering the jars.

7. Process for 15 minutes, adjusting for altitude. Remove the jars from the canner and cool.

Spicy Pickled Okra

- 2 pounds fresh, young okra (small pods are best)
- 1 quart white vinegar
- 6 tablespoons pickling salt
- 8 cloves garlic, chopped
- 16 fresh hot peppers
- ¼ cup whole mustard seed
- ¼ cup whole dill seed
- 5 pint jars, lids, and bands

1. Fill the canner with enough water to cover the jars. Boil the water, reduce the heat to low, place the jars in the water, and simmer until ready to use. Prepare lids and bands by simmering them over low heat in a small saucepan.

2. Wash the okra and trim the stems, leaving the caps. Soak in a bowl of ice water for 1 hour and then pat dry.

3. In a large nonmetallic pot, combine the vinegar, salt, garlic, hot peppers, mustard seed, and dill seed. Bring contents to a boil and simmer for 5 minutes.

4. Pack the okra evenly into the jars. Fill with hot pickling liquid, leaving ½ inch of headspace.

5. Remove air bubbles, wipe rims, center the lids, and screw on the bands and adjust until they are fingertip tight.

6. Place the jars in the canner and bring to a boil. Make sure there is at least 1 inch of water covering the jars.

7. Process for 10 minutes, adjusting for altitude. Remove the jars from the canner and cool.

8. The jars need to mature for about 4 weeks before they're ready to use.

Simple Bread-and-Butter Pickles

- 4 pounds cucumbers, sliced
- 8 small onions, sliced
- ½ cup pickling salt
- 5 cups granulated sugar
- 4 cups white vinegar
- 2 tablespoons mustard seed
- 2 teaspoons celery seed
- 1½ teaspoons ground turmeric
- ½ teaspoon ground cloves
- 7 pint jars, lids, and bands

1. Fill the canner with enough water to cover the jars. Boil the water, reduce the heat to low, place the jars in the water, and simmer until ready to use. Prepare lids and bands by simmering them over low heat in a small saucepan.

2. In a large container with a lid, combine the cucumbers, onions, and salt. Cover with crushed ice and mix well. Let stand for 3 hours. Drain, rinse, and drain again.

3. In a heavy saucepan with a lid, combine the sugar, vinegar, and seasonings. Bring to a boil.

4. Once boiling, add the cucumber mixture, and then return to a boil. When the mixture has boiled for 1 minute, remove the pot from the heat.

5. Carefully ladle the mixture into jars, leaving ½ inch of headspace.

6. Remove air bubbles, wipe rims, center the lids, and screw on the bands and adjust until they are fingertip tight.

7. Place the jars in the canner and bring to a boil. Make sure there is at least 1 inch of water covering the jars.

8. Process for 15 minutes, adjusting for altitude. Remove the jars from the canner and cool.

Pickled Peaches

- 1 cup white vinegar
- 2 cups granulated sugar
- 2 cinnamon sticks, broken in half
- 14 firm, slightly underripe peaches, peeled and sliced
- 2 teaspoons ground cloves

1. Fill the canner with enough water to cover the jars. Boil the water, reduce the heat to low, place the jars in the water, and simmer until ready to use. Prepare lids and bands by simmering them over low heat in a small saucepan.

2. Bring the vinegar, sugar, and cinnamon sticks to a boil in a saucepan.

3. Pack the peaches into the jars. The cinnamon sticks may be added to the jars for extra flavor or removed and discarded if desired. Add the syrup, leaving ½ inch of headspace.

4. Remove air bubbles, wipe rims, center the lids, and screw on the bands and adjust until they are fingertip tight.

5. Place the jars in the canner and bring to a boil. Make sure there is at least 1 inch of water covering the jars.

6. Process for 10 minutes, adjusting for altitude. Remove the jars from the canner and cool.

9

SALSAS AND RELISHES

Making your own salsas and relishes is both simple and fun. It's easy to exercise your creativity and customize flavors to your family's liking once you get the hang of making your own.

When making your own tomato recipes, be sure to use produce that is at its peak of ripeness. Processing will not improve the flavor of underripe tomatoes. With fruit salsas such as mango or peach, you can use fruit that is just slightly underripe, as you want the fruit to hold its shape somewhat, and you don't want the salsa to be too sweet.

Chunky Cranberry Sauce

- 4 cups granulated sugar
- 4 cups water
- 8 cups fresh cranberries
- 3 tablespoons fresh orange zest
- 4 pint jars, lids, and bands

1. Fill the canner with enough water to cover the jars. Boil the water, reduce the heat to low, place the jars in the water, and simmer until ready to use. Prepare lids and bands by simmering them over low heat in a small saucepan.

2. In a stockpot, combine the sugar and water and bring to a boil, stirring until the sugar is dissolved. Keep at a rolling boil for about 5 minutes, and then add the cranberries. Bring the mixture back to a boil and reduce heat to a simmer for about 15 minutes, until the cranberries start to burst and the liquid begins to thicken and "sheets" off the spoon. Add the orange zest.

3. Remove from the heat and ladle carefully into the jars, leaving ½ of headspace.

4. Remove air bubbles, wipe rims, center the lids, and screw on the bands and adjust until they are fingertip tight.

5. Place the jars in the canner and bring to a boil. Make sure there is at least 1 inch of water covering the jars.

6. Process for 15 minutes, adjusting for altitude. Remove the jars from the canner and cool.

Green Chow-Chow

- 12 green tomatoes, cored and quartered
- 3 medium green bell peppers, seeded and chopped
- 3 medium red bell peppers, seeded and chopped
- 3 medium yellow bell peppers, seeded and chopped
- 3 medium onions, peeled and quartered
- 1 cup fresh jalapeños, stemmed and chopped
- 8 cups water
- ¾ cup pickling salt
- 2½ cups white vinegar
- 6 half-pint jars, lids, and bands

1. Fill the canner with enough water to cover the jars. Boil the water, reduce the heat to low, place the jars in the water, and simmer until ready to use. Prepare lids and bands by simmering them over low heat in a small saucepan.

2. In a food processor, pulse the tomatoes about 10 times. Pour the tomatoes into a nonreactive stockpot.

3. Add the bell peppers, onions, and jalapeños to the processor, and pulse about 10 times as well. Add the mixture to the tomatoes.

4. Stir in the water, pickling salt, and vinegar. Over high heat, bring everything to a boil. Reduce the heat and simmer for about 20 minutes.

5. Remove from the heat and ladle into the jars, leaving ½ inch of headspace.

6. Remove air bubbles, wipe rims, center the lids, and screw on the bands and adjust until they are fingertip tight.

7. Place the jars in the canner and bring to a boil. Make sure there is at least 1 inch of water covering the jars.

8. Process for 15 minutes, adjusting for altitude. Remove the jars from the canner and cool.

9. Store in a cool dark place. It takes about 2 weeks to perfectly age, and then it is ready to eat.

Canned Plum Tomatoes

- 5 pounds plum tomatoes
- 16 quarts water
- 4 cups tomato paste
- 2 tablespoons bottled lemon juice or ¼ teaspoon citric acid per pint

- 8 leaves fresh basil
- 8 tablespoons olive oil
- 8 pint jars, lids, and bands

---

1. Fill the canner with enough water to cover the jars. Boil the water, reduce the heat to low, place the jars in the water, and simmer until ready to use. Prepare lids and bands by simmering them over low heat in a small saucepan.

2. Bring two pots, each filled with 8 quarts of water to a boil. Fill a bowl full of ice water. Place half of the tomatoes in one of the pots of boiling water for 1 minute.

3. Remove the tomatoes from the boiling water and place in the ice water. Repeat with the other half of tomatoes.

4. Heat the tomato paste in a saucepan until hot to the touch.

5. Add the lemon juice or citric acid to each jar.

6. When the tomatoes are cool enough to handle, carefully remove the skins and place in the jars.

7. When jars are filled with tomatoes, pour the hot tomato paste in, top each jar with a fresh basil leaf and 1 tablespoon of olive oil. Leave ½ inch of headspace.

8. Remove air bubbles, wipe rims, center the lids, and screw on the bands and adjust until they are fingertip tight.

9. Place the jars in the canner and bring to a boil. Make sure there is at least 1 inch of water covering the jars.

10. Process for 15 minutes, adjusting for altitude. Remove the jars from the canner and cool.

Fresh Tomato Salsa

- 12 pounds tomatoes, cored and quartered
- 4 green bell peppers, chopped
- 3 large yellow onions, chopped
- 1 red bell pepper, chopped
- 1 stalk celery, chopped
- 15 large cloves garlic, chopped
- 4–5 jalapeño peppers, seeded and chopped
- 2 (12-ounce) cans tomato paste
- 1¾ cups white vinegar
- ½ cup granulated sugar
- ¼ cup pickling salt
- ¼ –½ teaspoon hot pepper sauce
- 10 pint jars, lids, and bands

1. Place all of the tomatoes in a large stockpot, and cook over medium heat for 20 minutes. Drain the tomatoes, reserving 2 cups of the liquid, and return just the tomatoes to the pot.

2. Stir in the green peppers, onions, red pepper, celery, garlic, jalapeños, tomato paste, vinegar, sugar, pickling salt, hot pepper sauce, and reserved tomato liquid. Bring the mixture to a boil and reduce the heat to medium-low.

3. Simmer uncovered for 1 hour, stirring frequently.

4. Fill the canner with enough water to cover the jars. Boil the water, reduce the heat to low, place the jars in the water, and simmer until ready to use.

5. Ladle the hot mixture into the canning jars, leaving ¼ inch of headspace.

6. Remove air bubbles, wipe the rims, center the lids, and screw on the bands and adjust until they are fingertip tight.

7. Place the jars in the canner and bring to a boil. Make sure there is at least 1 inch of water covering the jars.

8. Process for 20 minutes, adjusting for altitude. Remove the jars from the canner and cool.

Homemade Tomato Paste

- 8 quarts fleshy tomatoes
- 2 cups chopped red bell peppers
- 2 bay leaves
- 2 tablespoons dried oregano
- 1 tablespoon dried basil
- 1 tablespoon granulated sugar, if your tomatoes are really acidic
- 1 teaspoon pickling salt
- 1 whole clove garlic
- ½ cup fresh or bottled lemon juice
- 9 half-pint jars, lids, and bands

1. Fill the canner with enough water to cover the jars. Boil the water, reduce the heat to low, place the jars in the water, and simmer until ready to use. Prepare lids and bands by simmering them over low heat in a small saucepan.

2. Quickly blanch the tomatoes in boiling water for no more than 40 seconds, and then toss immediately into ice water. When cooled, peel the skins off the tomatoes. (If you'd like to skip this step, you can press the paste through a sieve after cooking.)

3. For the smoothest texture, put the tomatoes into a blender or food processor.

4. In a large saucepan, combine the tomatoes, bell peppers, bay leaves, oregano, basil, sugar, and salt into a large saucepan. Simmer for 1 hour. (This can also be done in a slow cooker on high heat for 1 hour, but be sure to stir occasionally.)

5. Push the cooked mixture through a fine strainer or sieve, and return to the saucepan. Cook for about 2½ hours more, until the mixture is a paste. Stir frequently or the paste will stick to the pan.

6. Pour the paste into the jars, leaving ½ inch of headspace. Add ½ teaspoon of lemon juice into each jar, leaving ¼ inch of headspace. Lemon juice prevents spoilage and helps seal the color and flavor.

7. Remove air bubbles, wipe rims, center the lids, and screw on the bands and adjust until they are fingertip tight.

8. Place the jars in the canner and bring to a boil. Make sure there is at least 1 inch of water covering the jars.

9. Process for 45 minutes, adjusting for altitude. Remove the jars from the canner and cool.

10

GETTING STARTED WITH PRESSURE CANNING

The potential for the presence of the bacteria *Clostridium botulinum* in low-acid foods makes it unsafe to preserve them using the water-bath method. This is because the 212 degrees F that a water bath typically reaches isn't hot enough to kill the bacteria. High-acid foods aren't at risk for *C. botulinum*, because the acidic environment isn't conducive to its growth. However, to safely preserve low-acid foods, they must be processed at a temperature no less than 240 degrees F.

If low-acid ingredients are mixed with high-acid ingredients such as in stocks, stews, or soups (e.g., when meat is matched with tomatoes), the pH of the acidic food is lowered sufficiently to make the entire recipe a low-acid food that needs to be pressure canned.

Pressure canning is the safest method of canning for low-acid foods such as meats, poultry, seafood, and vegetables. Although you need to be careful, pressure canning is easy to learn, so don't stress; by the time you're finished here, you will be pressure canning like a pro. The following checklist will help you get organized.

+ Prepper's Checklist   Pressure Canning

- [ ] Weighted- or dial-gauge pressure canner
- [ ] Rack for the bottom of the pressure canner
- [ ] Jar lifter (tongs used to lift hot jars from the canner)
- [ ] Jars (½ pint, pint, or quart sizes)
- [ ] Canning funnel
- [ ] New lids for each jar
- [ ] Bands for each jar
- [ ] Clean dish towels for wiping jar rims
- [ ] Clean dish towels for cooling the hot jars
- [ ] Butter knife or thin spatula for removing air bubbles
- [ ] Watch or kitchen timer
- [ ] Marker and labels

Basic Instructions for Pressure Canning

1. Wash and heat your jars and lids as instructed in the water-bath method section. Be sure that you don't boil your lids, as it may damage the seals. Be very observant with your jars and bands. Check for cracks, dents, uneven threads, or other signs of damage, and throw out any that are imperfect.

2. Again, it's best to be fully organized and ready to go, so prepare all your ingredients and your canner beforehand. Remember to leave the jars and lids in the hot water or dishwasher until ready to fill them.

3. Don't overtighten your lids—remember that you want to let the air escape from the jars to create an environment unfriendly to pathogens. Just fingertip-tight is tight enough.

4. Leave the proper amount of headspace as dictated in the recipe. If you leave too much, all of the air may not be forced out during processing, and if you don't leave enough, your product may boil up and get between the seal and the jar, prohibiting a seal from forming.

5. For the same reason, do your best to eliminate as many bubbles as possible.

6. Just as with water-bath canning, you want to have a small pot of water simmering on the side in case you need a little more hot water to cover the jars. Don't ever pour cold water over hot jars, because they can and will explode, or at least break.

7. Once you have the jars in the canner, cover them with water and secure the canner's lid, making sure that it seals properly. Don't set the gauge over the vent port yet. Turn the heat on high with the vent open, and wait for steam to shoot steadily out before you put on the gauge. After you put on the gauge, the canner will begin to pressurize.

8. Begin on medium to high heat until you reach the right pressure, and then adjust the temperature back to where the gauge's dial remains in the correct zone or the weight continues to jiggle.

9. Be sure to set a timer for the recommended processing time stated in your recipe because pressure canning cooks at a much faster rate than standard boiling. Start timing when the weight starts to

jiggle or the gauge reads the correct pressure. When the timer is up, remove the canner from the heat and let cool.

10. Make sure you're canning with the pressure indicated in the recipe and adjusted for your altitude. Most foods are canned at either 10 pounds of pressure using a weighted gauge or 11 pounds of pressure using a dial gauge. You will have to adjust the pressure for altitude. See the following altitude chart. You'll also find an altitude chart at the back of the book for selected cities in the United States and Canada.

Altitude in Feet	Altitude in Meters	Weighted-Gauge Pounds / Dial-Gauge Pounds
0 – 1,000	0 – 305	10 / 11
1,001 – 2,000	306 – 609	15 / 11
2,001 – 4,000	610 – 1,219	15 / 12
4,001 – 6,000	1,220 – 1,829	15 / 13
6,001 – 8,000	1,830 – 2,438	15 / 14
8,001 – 10,000	2,439 – 3,048	15 / 15

11. Very important: **do not remove the gauge until all pressure is relieved from the canner.** It is important to allow the pressure within the canner to return to 0 naturally.

12. After following the recommended steps in your manual to release the pressure, remove the weight gauge and unlock the lid. Tilt the lid away from you to prevent being burned by any leftover steam inside the canner.

13. Place a thick folded towel on your counter, and remove the jars (using tongs or lifter) without tilting them. Place them upright on

the towel to allow the jars to cool. Otherwise, breaking and cracking can occur.

14. Don't touch the jars for at least 12 to 24 hours, and don't turn them upside down. Again, just as in the water-bath instructions, do not attempt to readjust the lids, as this may damage the strength of the seal.

15. If you have food that doesn't seal, refrigerate it immediately and consume within a few days.

Prep Tip To keep jars from falling over or floating around as you simmer them during sterilization, fill them with water.

Basic Steps for Pressure-Canning Soups

- If you are canning a soup with dry beans, cook the beans first for a few minutes ahead of time. Simply cover the beans with a few inches of water in a pot. Bring to a boil, simmer for about 2 minutes, remove from the heat, and let them soak for about an hour. Then drain and continue with your soup.

- First cook any meats and vegetables going into the soup as instructed by the recipe. Then combine all ingredients and add the broth or whatever liquid you are using as a base. Finally, add seasonings and spices. Bring to a boil and simmer for 5 minutes.

- When canning, you do not want to add any dairy, pasta, thickeners, or rice. These will have to be added later when you serve the soup.

- Fill the jars, leaving 1 inch of headspace. The easiest way to do this is by filling the jars with the solids of the soup first; that way, they will be evenly distributed among the jars. Then fill the jars with the liquids. If you run out of liquids before the jars are full, that's okay. Simply heat some more stock or broth if you are lacking a good amount, or if you are lacking only a little bit at the tops, add hot water to top them off.

- Clean the rims of the jars well and secure the lids and bands. Follow the pressure-canning instructions discussed earlier and in the instruction booklet that came with your pressure canner.

- When processing pints, you want to allow 60 minutes of processing time; with quarts, 75 minutes. If there is any seafood in the soup, you will need to extend the process time to 100 minutes, for both pints and quarts.

- Don't forget altitude adjustments.

11

PRESSURE CANNING RECIPES

Fresh-Canned Corn

• 20 fresh picked ears of corn, dehusked	• 4 teaspoons salt
	• 8 pint jars, lids, and bands

1. Prepare your jars by bringing them to a boil in a large pot. Once they reach a boil, reduce the heat to low, and allow them to simmer until you're ready to use them. Prepare the lids and bands by simmering (not boiling) them over low heat in a small saucepan.

2. Prepare your canner by filling it with 2 to 3 inches of water and bringing it to a boil over high heat.

3. Fill another large pot with water and bring to a boil. Add the whole ears of corn (in batches if needed) and blanch for 3 minutes. Remove from the water and place in a bowl of cold water.

4. Using a corn cobber or sharp paring knife, stand an ear of corn up with the wide end at the bottom, holding it firmly at the narrow end. Cut the rows of kernels off about three-quarters of the way to the cob. Do not scrape the cob. As you go, swipe the cut kernels into a large container. Repeat with each cob.

5. For raw pack: Once all of the corn has been cut, bring another large pot of water to a boil and allow it to continue boiling until you're ready to use it. Loosely pack the corn into the jars, leaving 1 inch of headspace. Add ½ teaspoon of salt to each jar. Pour in enough boiling water to cover, leaving 1 inch of headspace.

6. For hot pack: Use a quart jar or measuring pitcher to measure the corn kernels. Put all of the corn into a large pot, and for every quart of corn, add 1 cup of cold water. Bring to a boil and cook for 5 minutes. Pack the corn loosely into the jars, leaving 1 inch of headspace. Add ½ teaspoon of salt to each jar. Pour in enough of the cooking water to cover, leaving 1 inch of headspace.

7. Remove air bubbles, wipe rims, center the lids, and screw on the bands and adjust until they are fingertip tight. Place the jars in the canner.

8. Cover, vent, and pressurize the canner according to its manufacturer's directions.

9. For both raw- and hot-pack methods, process the corn for 55 minutes at 11 pounds of pressure, adjusting for altitude. Remove the canner from the burner and allow to cool before removing the jars.

Canned Beets

- 10 pounds small to medium red beets
- 5 teaspoons salt
- 10 pint jars, lids, and bands

---

1. Wash the beets well. Cut the stems to about 2 inches, but leave the taproot on so the color won't drain out of the beets.

2. Boil the beets in a large stockpot until the skins are loose and easy to peel. This takes about 10 minutes. One way to check if the beets are done is to scrape a spoon or butter knife across the side of a beet; if the skin peels off, then they are done. (During this phase, it's best to arrange the beets according to size. If you have mostly large beets, take the small ones out and replace them with one proportionate to the rest. Larger beets will also take longer to boil.)

3. Prepare your jars by bringing them to a boil in a large pot. Once they reach a boil, reduce the heat to low, and allow them to simmer until you're ready to use them. Prepare the lids and bands by simmering (not boiling) them over low heat in a small saucepan.

4. Prepare your canner by filling it with 2 to 3 inches of water and bringing it to a boil over high heat.

5. When the beets are done boiling, remove them from the water and let them cool. When the beets are cool enough to touch, begin peeling the skins off (you may want to use gloves). Cut off the tops and taproots.

6. Slice or chop the beets to the desired size. If you have small beets, you can leave them whole, but larger beets need to be sliced or cut into pieces. Pack into jars, leaving 1 inch of headspace.

7. Add ½ teaspoon of salt to each jar.

8. Fill each jar with boiling water, leaving 1 inch of headspace.

9. Remove air bubbles, wipe rims, center the lids, and screw on the bands and adjust until they are fingertip tight. Place the jars in the canner.

10. Cover, vent, and pressurize the canner according to its manufacturer's directions.

11. Process for at least 30 minutes at 11 pounds of pressure, adjusting for altitude. Remove the canner from the burner and allow to cool before removing the jars.

Canned Green Beans

- 14 pounds green beans
- 7 teaspoons salt

- 14 pint jars, lids, and bands

---

1. Prepare the jars by bringing them to a boil in a large pot. Once they reach a boil, reduce the heat to low, and allow them to simmer until you're ready to use them. Prepare the lids and bands by simmering (not boiling) them over low heat in a small saucepan.

2. Prepare your canner by filling it with 2 to 3 inches of water and bringing it to a boil over high heat.

3. Fill another large pot with water and bring to a boil. Continue boiling until ready to use.

4. Wash the green beans and trim off the ends. If there are strings, remove them with your fingertips or a small paring knife.

5. For raw pack: Pack the beans into the jars, leaving 1 inch of headspace. Once all of the jars are packed, pour in enough boiling water to cover, leaving 1 inch of headspace.

6. For hot pack: Place the beans into the boiling water, reduce the heat to medium and simmer for 5 minutes. Use a slotted spoon to pack into jars, leaving 1 inch of headspace. Add enough of the cooking water to cover, leaving 1 inch of headspace.

7. Add ½ teaspoon of salt to each jar.

8. Remove air bubbles, wipe rims, center the lids, and screw on the bands and adjust until they are fingertip tight. Place the jars in the canner.

9. Cover, vent, and pressurize the canner according to its manufacturer's directions.

10. For both raw- and hot-pack methods, process the jars for 20 minutes at 11 pounds of pressure, adjusting for altitude. Remove the canner from the burner and allow to cool before removing the jars.

Candied Carrots

These slightly sweet nuggets are a hit even with kids who don't like carrots. In a survival situation, the extra carbs will provide more energy.

- 10 cups water
- ¼ cup brown sugar
- 2½ tablespoons ground cinnamon

- 18 pounds of carrots, peeled and sliced into ½-inch slices
- 1 tablespoon salt
- 7 quart jars, lids, and bands

1. Prepare the jars by bringing them to a boil in a large pot. Once they reach a boil, reduce the heat to low, and allow them to simmer until you're ready to use them. Prepare the lids and bands by simmering (not boiling) them over low heat in a small saucepan.

2. Prepare your canner by filling it with 2 to 3 inches of water and bringing it to a boil over high heat.

3. Combine water, brown sugar, and cinnamon in a saucepan, and bring to a boil.

4. Stuff as many carrots into each jar as possible. Ladle the hot sugar water equally into each jar, leaving ½ inch of headspace. If you don't have enough liquid to bring it to that level, finish filling with hot water.

5. Remove air bubbles, wipe rims, center the lids, and screw on the bands and adjust until they are fingertip tight. Place the jars in the canner.

6. Cover, vent, and pressurize the canner according to its manufacturer's directions.

7. Process for 30 minutes at 11 pounds of pressure, adjusting for altitude. Remove the canner from the burner and allow to cool before removing the jars.

Candied Sweet Potatoes

- 28 medium sweet potatoes
- 10 cups water
- ½ cup brown sugar
- 2 teaspoons salt
- 2 tablespoons ground cinnamon
- 1 tablespoon pumpkin pie spice or allspice
- 7 quart jars, lids, and bands

1. Prepare the jars by bringing them to a boil in a large pot. Once they reach a boil, reduce the heat to low, and allow them to simmer until you're ready to use them. Prepare the lids and bands by simmering (not boiling) them over low heat in a small saucepan.

2. Prepare your canner by filling it with 2 to 3 inches of water and bringing it to a boil over high heat.

3. Clean the sweet potatoes, chop into 1-inch chucks or wedges, and stuff tightly in the jars.

4. Bring the water, sugar, salt, and spices to a boil in a saucepan, and then distribute evenly between each jar, leaving ½ inch of headspace. If you don't have enough liquid, fill with boiling water.

5. Remove air bubbles, wipe rims, center the lids, and screw on the bands and adjust until they are fingertip tight. Place the jars in the canner.

6. Cover, vent, and pressurize the canner according to its manufacturer's directions.

7. Process for 40 minutes at 11 pounds of pressure, adjusting for altitude. Remove the canner from the burner and allow to cool before removing the jars.

Mushrooms and Onions

- 4 pounds sliced mushrooms
- 14 medium onions, skinned, sliced, and ringed
- 2 tablespoons salt
- 7 quart jars, lids, and bands

---

1. Prepare the jars by bringing them to a boil in a large pot. Once they reach a boil, reduce the heat to low, and allow them to simmer until you're ready to use them. Prepare the lids and bands by simmering (not boiling) them over low heat in a small saucepan.

2. Prepare your canner by filling it with 2 to 3 inches of water and bringing it to a boil over high heat.

3. Blanch mushrooms and onions for 5 minutes.

4. Pack the mushrooms and the onions in the jars and add 1 teaspoon of salt per jar. Cover with boiling water, leaving ½ inch of headspace.

5. Remove air bubbles, wipe rims, center the lids, and screw on the bands and adjust until they are fingertip tight. Place the jars in the canner.

6. Cover, vent, and pressurize the canner according to its manufacturer's directions.

7. Process for 30 minutes at 11 pounds of pressure, adjusting for altitude. Remove the canner from the burner and allow to cool before removing the jars.

White Potatoes

Great for slicing, mashing, frying, or tossing in a soup, potatoes are a great survival food.

- 9 pounds of potatoes, peeled if desired, and cubed
- 7 teaspoons salt
- 7 quart jars, lids, and bands

1. Prepare the jars by bringing them to a boil in a large pot. Once they reach a boil, reduce the heat to low, and allow them to simmer until you're ready to use them. Prepare the lids and bands by simmering (not boiling) them over low heat in a small saucepan.

2. Prepare your canner by filling it with 2 to 3 inches of water and bringing it to a boil over high heat.

3. Pack potatoes as tightly as possible into the jars. Add 1 teaspoon of salt to each jar. Add enough boiling water to fill, leaving ½ inch headspace.

4. Remove air bubbles, wipe rims, center the lids, and screw on the bands and adjust until they are fingertip tight. Place the jars in the canner.

5. Cover, vent, and pressurize the canner according to its manufacturer's directions.

6. Process for 40 minutes at 11 pounds of pressure, adjusting for altitude. Remove the canner from the burner and allow to cool before removing the jars.

Simple Beef Stock

Having stocks in a survival situation can be vital for recovering from illness, adding flavor and nutrition to foods, and helping avoid food fatigue.

- 8 pounds of meaty beef bones
- 16 cups water
- 2 medium onions, finely chopped
- 2 carrots, sliced
- 2 stalks celery, sliced
- 1 bay leaf
- 2 teaspoons salt
- 8 pint jars, lids, and bands

1. Prepare the jars by bringing them to a boil in a large pot. Once they reach a boil, reduce the heat to low, and allow them to simmer until you're ready to use them. Prepare the lids and bands by simmering (not boiling) them over low heat in a small saucepan.

2. Prepare your canner by filling it with 2 to 3 inches of water and bringing it to a boil over high heat.

3. Place the bones and water into a large pot, and boil over high heat. When boiling, reduce the heat to almost low and remove any foam as it forms.

4. Add the onions, carrots, celery, bay leaf, and salt. Cover and gently boil for 3 hours. For a strong reduced broth, boil longer.

5. Spoon out the beef bones and toss. Strain the stock through a fine sieve or cheesecloth-lined strainer. Discard vegetables and bay leaf. Allow the stock to cool until the fat solidifies, and then remove it.

6. Heat the stock to a boil again and ladle carefully using a funnel, filling one jar at a time. Leave 1 inch of headspace.

7. Remove air bubbles, wipe rims, center the lids, and screw on the bands and adjust until they are fingertip tight. Place the jars in the canner.

8. Cover, vent, and pressurize the canner according to its manufacturer's directions.

9. Process for 20 minutes at 11 pounds of pressure, adjusting for altitude. Remove the canner from the burner and allow to cool before removing the jars.

Beef Tips

These are great for use in soups and stews. You can use venison, bison, elk, moose, or any other red meat in this simple recipe. The raw-pack method is used here because then you can season it as you want it. If you use gamey meat such as venison, drop in a bouillon cube and you'll never know it's not beef!

- 25 cups cubed meat (3½ cups per quart jar)
- 7 teaspoons of salt
- 7 quart jars, lids, and bands

---

1. Prepare the jars by bringing them to a boil in a large pot. Once they reach a boil, reduce the heat to low, and allow them to simmer until you're ready to use them. Prepare the lids and bands by simmering (not boiling) them over low heat in a small saucepan.

2. Prepare your canner by filling it with 2 to 3 inches of water and bringing it to a boil over high heat.

3. Pack the meat into the jars as tightly as possible, leaving 1 inch of headspace. Add the salt.

4. Remove air bubbles, wipe rims, center the lids, and screw on the bands and adjust until they are fingertip tight. Place the jars in the canner.

5. Process for 90 minutes at 11 pounds of pressure, adjusting for altitude. Remove the canner from the burner and allow to cool before removing the jars.

Chicken Stock

- 10 pounds uncooked chicken or turkey pieces and/or bones (skin and fat discarded)
- 2 onions, peeled and coarsely chopped
- 2 carrots, rinsed and cut into chunks
- 4 stalks celery, leafy tops left on, rinsed and cut into chunks
- 1 cup fresh parsley sprigs
- 10 black peppercorns
- 2 bay leaves
- 2 sprigs fresh thyme
- 20 cups water
- 2 teaspoons salt
- 5 quart jars, lids, and bands

1. In a large stockpot, over medium-high heat, combine chicken, onions, carrots, celery, parsley, peppercorns, bay leaves, and thyme.

2. Cover ingredients with the water. Bring to a light boil (a simmer), reduce the heat, keeping a simmer, and cook for 2 hours. The broth will have a golden color and smell richly of chicken. Remove any foam on the surface while simmering. If the liquids begin to reduce too much, simply add more cold water, just enough to cover the solids.

3. Strain the vegetables and spices, and discard the solids.

4. Stir the broth occasionally while letting it cool for 15 minutes. Then cover and chill until the broth is cold, anywhere from 6 hours to a full day. When the fat on the top is firm, spoon it away and discard or store in a jar for other cooking.

5. Prepare the jars by bringing them to a boil in a large pot. Once they reach a boil, reduce the heat to low, and allow them to simmer until you're ready to use them. Prepare the lids and bands by simmering (not boiling) them over low heat in a small saucepan.

6. Prepare your canner by filling it with 2 to 3 inches of water and bringing it to a boil over high heat.

7. Pour the broth into the jars, leaving 1 inch of headspace.

8. Remove air bubbles, wipe rims, center the lids, and screw on the bands and adjust until they are fingertip tight. Place the jars in the canner.

9. Process for 75 minutes at 11 pounds of pressure, adjusting for altitude. Remove the canner from the burner and allow to cool before removing the jars.

Ground Meat Base Mix

This basic mixture is a great foundation for any number of meals, from soups and stews to casseroles and tacos. Having it already cooked and on hand will make so many mealtimes easier and less stressful.

- 8 pounds ground beef, lamb, pork, chicken, or turkey
- 5 teaspoons salt
- 2 teaspoons freshly ground black pepper
- 2 medium yellow onions, chopped
- 4 large garlic cloves, chopped
- 3 cups beef or chicken broth
- 7 quart jars, lids, and bands

1. Prepare your jars by bringing them to a boil in a large pot. Once they reach a boil, reduce the heat to low, and allow them to simmer until you're ready to use them. Prepare the lids and bands by simmering (not boiling) them over low heat in a small saucepan.

2. Prepare your canner by filling it with 2 to 3 inches of water and bringing it to a boil over high heat.

3. In a large bowl, combine the meat, salt, and pepper, mixing well with clean hands. Working in batches, if necessary, brown the meat over medium-heat in a large skillet. Stir frequently with a spatula or wooden spoon, breaking up the meat as it cooks to a crumbly texture.

4. Once the meat is gently browned, add the onions and garlic and sauté for another 3 to 4 minutes or until the onions are transparent. Reduce the heat to low.

5. In a large saucepan, heat the broth over medium-high heat until it boils and continue a soft boil.

6. Pack the hot meat loosely into the jars, leaving 1 inch of headspace. Add enough hot broth to cover, leaving 1 inch of headspace.

7. Remove air bubbles, wipe rims, center the lids, and screw on the bands and adjust until they are fingertip tight. Place the jars in the canner.

8. Cover, vent, and pressurize the canner according to its manufacturer's directions.

9. Process for 90 minutes at 11 pounds of pressure, adjusting for altitude. Remove the canner from the burner, and allow to cool before removing the jars.

Chicken with Gravy

You can make a lot of great meals starting with just cooked chicken and a little pan gravy. Use this as the starter for chicken potpie, chicken and dumplings, chicken noodle casserole, or anything else you and your family enjoy. This recipe works equally well with turkey.

- 10 pounds bone-in chicken breasts or thighs
- 3 tablespoons olive or canola oil
- 4 teaspoons salt
- 2 teaspoons freshly ground black pepper
- 8 tablespoons reserved chicken drippings
- 8 tablespoons flour
- 6 cups chicken broth or stock
- 1 teaspoon dried rosemary
- 1 teaspoon dried thyme
- 7 quart jars, lids, and bands

1. Prepare your jars by bringing them to a boil in a large pot. Once they reach a boil, reduce the heat to low, and allow them to simmer until you're ready to use them. Prepare the lids and bands by simmering (not boiling) them over low heat in a small saucepan.

2. Prepare your canner by filling it with 2 to 3 inches of water and bringing it to a boil over high heat.

3. Preheat the oven to 375 degrees F.

4. Brush the chicken with the oil, and then season on all sides with the salt and pepper. Place into one or two large baking dishes, and bake for 40 to 45 minutes or until the chicken is cooked through. Set aside in the casserole dishes for 10 to 15 minutes or until cool enough to handle.

5. Remove all of the meat and skin from the chicken. Reserve bones and scraps for stock if desired.

6. Measure out 8 tablespoons of chicken drippings from the pans and place in a large saucepan. Bring to a boil over medium-high heat.

7. Once the drippings boil, quickly add the flour, whisking constantly until it resembles a paste.

8. Slowly stir in the broth or stock, and whisk until smooth. Add the rosemary and thyme. Bring back to a boil and then simmer for 20 minutes.

9. Pack the meat loosely into the jars, leaving 2 inches of headspace. Add enough gravy to cover and leave 1 inch of headspace.

10. Remove air bubbles, wipe rims, center the lids, and screw on the bands and adjust until they are fingertip tight. Place the jars in the canner.

11. Cover, vent, and pressurize the canner according to its manufacturer's directions.

12. Process for 90 minutes at 11 pounds of pressure, adjusting for altitude. Remove the canner from the burner, and allow to cool before removing the jars.

Meatless Spaghetti Sauce

This basic spaghetti sauce is versatile enough to use as a pizza sauce, for pasta dishes, or on sub sandwiches. It's quick and easy to make, and it tastes wonderful.

- 30 pounds fresh tomatoes
- ¼ cup vegetable oil
- 1 cup chopped yellow onion
- 5 large garlic cloves, chopped
- 1 cup chopped green bell pepper
- 1 pound fresh mushrooms, sliced
- 4½ teaspoons salt
- 2 teaspoons freshly ground black pepper
- 4 tablespoons dried parsley
- 2 tablespoons dried oregano
- ¼ cup packed brown sugar
- 9 pint jars, lids, and bands

1. Prepare your jars by bringing them to a boil in a large pot. Once they reach a boil, reduce the heat to low, and allow them to simmer until you're ready to use them. Prepare lids and bands by simmering (not boiling) them over low heat in a small saucepan.

2. Prepare your canner by filling it with 2 to 3 inches of water and bringing it to a boil over high heat.

3. Bring a large pot of water to a boil over high heat.

4. Wash the tomatoes and plunge in boiling water for 30 seconds or until the skins begin to split. Dip immediately into icy cold water, and slip off the skins. Core and quarter the tomatoes.

5. In a large saucepan, bring the tomatoes to a boil over medium-high heat, stirring frequently. Boil for 20 minutes, uncovered. If you would like the sauce to be smoother, put the tomatoes through a food mill or sieve.

6. In a large saucepan, heat the vegetable oil over medium-high heat and sauté the onion, garlic, bell pepper, and mushrooms until tender. Combine the sautéed vegetables and the tomatoes, and add the salt, black pepper, and herbs. Once the sauce boils, stir in the brown sugar. Simmer uncovered, until reduced by about half.

7. Ladle the hot spaghetti sauce into the jars, leaving 1 inch of headspace.

8. Remove air bubbles, wipe rims, center the lids, and screw on the bands and adjust until they are fingertip tight. Place the jars in the canner.

9. Cover, vent, and pressurize the canner according to its manufacturer's directions.

10. Process for 20 minutes at 11 pounds of pressure, adjusting for altitude. Remove the canner from the burner, and allow to cool before removing the jars.

Vegetable Soup

This vegetable soup is a great one for using plenty of fresh vegetables when they're abundant in your garden or at their peak and priced low at the farmers' market.

- 8 cups peeled and chopped tomatoes
- 6 cups peeled and diced potatoes
- 6 cups sliced carrots
- 4 cups green beans, trimmed and cut into 1-inch pieces
- 4 cups uncooked corn kernels
- 2 cups 1-inch sliced celery
- 2 cups chopped yellow onions
- 6 cups water
- 2 teaspoons salt
- 1 teaspoon freshly ground black pepper
- ½ cup chopped fresh parsley
- 1 tablespoon chopped fresh rosemary
- 7 quart jars, lids, and bands

1. Prepare your jars by bringing them to a boil in a large pot. Once they reach a boil, reduce the heat to low, and allow them to simmer until you're ready to use them. Prepare the lids and bands by simmering (not boiling) them over low heat in a small saucepan.

2. Prepare your canner by filling it with 2 to 3 inches of water and bringing it to a boil over high heat.

3. Combine all of the vegetables in a large stockpot over medium-high heat. Add the water. Season with salt and pepper, and stir well. Add in the herbs and stir.

4. Bring to a boil. Reduce the heat and simmer 25 minutes.

5. Ladle the hot soup into the jars, leaving 1 inch of headspace.

6. Remove air bubbles, wipe rims, center the lids, and screw on the bands and adjust until they are fingertip tight. Place the jars in the canner.

7. Cover, vent, and pressurize the canner according to its manufacturer's directions.

8. Process for 1 hour and 25 minutes at 10 pounds of pressure, adjusting for altitude. Remove the canner from the burner, and allow to cool before removing the jars.

Chicken Soup

This hearty chicken soup is a classic and a real favorite among home canners. This makes a wonderful gift for a new mother or someone who is ill. To make it even heartier, boil some egg noodles as you're reheating your soup and stir them into the soup at the end.

- 16 cups chicken stock
- 3 cups diced cooked chicken
- 1½ cups diced celery
- 1½ cups sliced carrots
- 1 cup diced onion
- 2 teaspoons salt
- 1 teaspoon freshly ground black pepper
- ½ cup chopped fresh parsley
- 2 tablespoons chopped fresh thyme
- 1½ teaspoons ground turmeric
- Chicken bouillon cubes (optional)
- 4 quart jars, lids, and bands

1. Prepare your jars by bringing them to a boil in a large pot. Once they reach a boil, reduce the heat to low, and allow them to simmer until you're ready to use them. Prepare the lids and bands by simmering (not boiling) them over low heat in a small saucepan.

2. Prepare your canner by filling it with 2 to 3 inches of water and bringing it to a boil over high heat.

3. In a large stockpot over medium-high heat, combine the chicken stock, chicken, celery, carrots, and onion. Bring to a boil, reduce the heat to medium, and add the salt, pepper, parsley, thyme, and turmeric, stirring well.

4. Cover and simmer for 30 minutes. Add bouillon cubes, if desired. Cook until the bouillon cubes are dissolved.

5. Ladle the hot soup into the jars, leaving 1 inch of headspace.

6. Remove air bubbles, wipe rims, center the lids, and screw on the bands and adjust until they are fingertip tight. Place the jars in the canner.

7. Cover, vent, and pressurize the canner according to its manufacturer's directions.

8. Process for 90 minutes at 10 pounds of pressure, adjusting for altitude. Remove the canner from the burner, and allow to cool before removing the jars.

Garden Fresh Veggie Soup

- 2 cups chopped baby carrots
- 2 baking potatoes, cut into cubes
- 1 small sweet onion, chopped
- 2 stalks celery, chopped
- One-half small head cabbage, chopped
- 2 cups chopped tomatoes
- 2 cups green beans, cut into ½-inch pieces
- 2½ quarts chicken broth
- 1 quart vegetable stock
- 2 cups water
- 1½ teaspoons dried basil
- Pinch of rubbed sage
- Pinch of dried thyme
- Salt to taste
- 8 pint jars, lids, and bands

1. Prepare your jars by bringing them to a boil in a large pot. Once they reach a boil, reduce the heat to low, and allow them to simmer until you're ready to use them. Prepare the lids and bands by simmering (not boiling) them over low heat in a small saucepan.

2. Prepare your canner by filling it with 2 to 3 inches of water and bringing it to a boil over high heat.

3. In a large stockpot over medium-high heat, combine all the ingredients except the salt and bring to a boil.

4. Cover, reduce the heat, and simmer 30 minutes. Season to taste with salt, if desired.

5. Ladle the hot soup into the jars, leaving 1 inch of headspace.

6. Remove air bubbles, wipe rims, center the lids, and screw on the bands and adjust until they are fingertip tight. Place the jars in the canner.

7. Cover, vent, and pressurize the canner according to its manufacturer's directions.

8. Process for 90 minutes at 10 pounds of pressure, adjusting for altitude. Remove the canner from the burner, and allow to cool before removing the jars.

Basic Vegetable Stock

- 1 tablespoon olive oil
- 1 large onion
- 2 stalks celery, including leaves
- 2 large carrots
- 1 bunch green onions, chopped in long sections
- 8 cloves garlic, minced
- 8 sprigs fresh parsley
- 6 sprigs fresh thyme
- 2 bay leaves
- 1 teaspoon salt
- 2 quarts water
- 3 quart jars, lids, and bands

1. Prepare your jars by bringing them to a boil in a large pot. Once they reach a boil, reduce the heat to low, and allow them to simmer until you're ready to use them. Prepare the lids and bands by simmering (not boiling) them over low heat in a small saucepan.

2. Prepare your canner by filling it with 2 to 3 inches of water and bringing it to a boil over high heat.

3. In a large stockpot over medium-high heat, combine all the ingredients and bring to a boil.

4. Cover, reduce the heat, and simmer for 30 minutes.

5. Strain the vegetables and spices, and discard the solids.

6. Ladle the hot stock into the jars, leaving 1 inch of headspace.

7. Remove air bubbles, wipe rims, center the lids, and screw on the bands and adjust until they are fingertip tight. Place the jars in the canner.

8. Cover, vent, and pressurize the canner according to its manufacturer's directions.

9. Process for 90 minutes at 10 pounds of pressure, adjusting for altitude. Remove the canner from the burner, and allow to cool before removing the jars.

Hearty Chili

People don't just like chili; they love it. Fortunately, it's a filling and economical meal that's great for lunch or dinner in any season. This chili is especially hearty and will be a big hit with your chili fans.

- 4 pounds boneless beef chuck roast or steak
- ¼ cup vegetable oil
- 3 cups chopped yellow onion
- 2 large garlic cloves, chopped
- 5 tablespoons chili powder
- 2 teaspoons cumin seed
- 2 teaspoons salt
- 1 teaspoon dried oregano
- ½ teaspoon freshly ground pepper
- ½ teaspoon ground coriander
- ½ teaspoon crushed red pepper
- 6 cups diced canned tomatoes with their juice
- 4 quart jars, lids, and bands

1. Prepare your jars by bringing them to a boil in a large pot. Once they reach a boil, reduce the heat to low, and allow them to simmer until you're ready to use them. Prepare the lids and bands by simmering (not boiling) them over low heat in a small saucepan.

2. Prepare your canner by filling it with 2 to 3 inches of water and bringing it to a boil over high heat.

3. Cut the beef chuck into ½-inch cubes, removing any sinew or extra fat.

4. Heat the oil in a large, heavy stockpot and lightly brown the meat. Add the onions and garlic, and continue to cook until the onions are slightly soft.

5. Add all of the seasoning and spices, and cook for 5 minutes. Stir in the diced tomatoes, together with their juices.

6. Bring to a boil, reduce the heat to medium, and simmer for 50 minutes, stirring occasionally.

7. Ladle the hot chili into the jars, leaving 1 inch of headspace.

8. Remove air bubbles, wipe rims, center the lids, and screw on the bands and adjust until they are fingertip tight. Place the jars in the canner.

9. Cover, vent, and pressurize the canner according to its manufacturer's directions.

10. Process for 90 minutes at 10 pounds of pressure, adjusting for altitude. Remove the canner from the burner, and allow to cool before removing the jars.

Drying and Storing Your Food

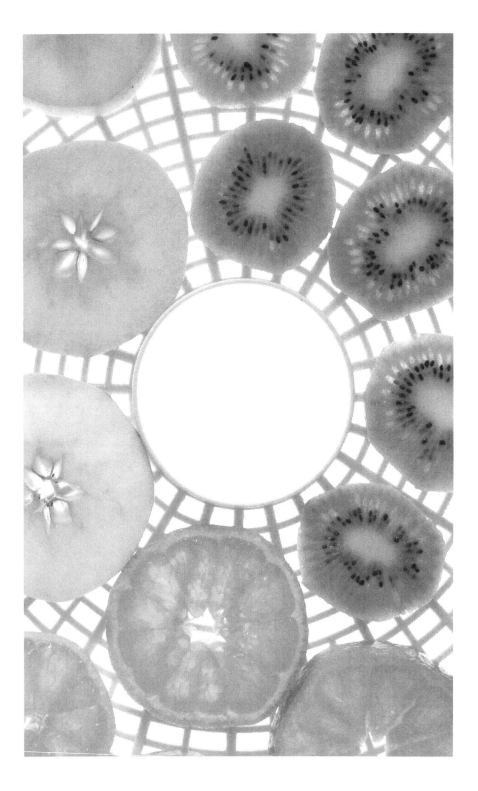

12

DRYING RECIPES:
PRODUCE, HERBS, AND MEATS

Drying is one of the earliest methods of preserving food, and it's a fairly simple process. Native Americans used it all the time to cure meat and preserve stores of food for winter use to keep from starving. This simple, effective method allows you to save food in a manner that's delicious, portable, and lasting: exactly the traits that you're looking for in survival situations. Little equipment is needed, and most of it you probably already own or can pick up for minimal cost. The secret to the way dry foods work is the moisture levels are so low that the organisms that spoil food are unable to live.

Drying is a great way to preserve your harvest. Dried fruits and vegetables are delicious, lightweight, easy to make, and packed with nutrition. One important thing about drying your own food is that it saves a great deal of space. For instance, you can store 16 to 20 dried tomatoes in one quart-sized jar or resealable bag.

Some people feel that drying doesn't compare to canning or freezing, because it doesn't quite preserve the texture, taste, appearance, or nutrition of the food. However, dried foods are great for nutrition on the go or for when other foods aren't available. In cases of emergency, dry foods may be extremely helpful when frozen or refrigerated foods are unavailable. Many people concerned with emergency preparedness prefer dry foods because they take up little space and don't require refrigeration.

Home drying methods largely depend upon what you're drying; it can be done several ways. Some methods use an oven (so use a well-ventilated, dry space) and others use a dehydrator. Many people prefer drying by the sun, but it requires very hot, dry air. Basically it depends largely on location, climate, and what tools are available.

Drying isn't hard, but it is time consuming. There are several different methods to choose from, with the top three described as follows.

Oven Drying

Although the most popular method, oven drying is also the most expensive. It takes a lot of electricity or gas due to the long drying times. It also doesn't have the best results flavor-wise. To use this method, preheat the oven to 145 degrees F, leaving the oven door open to allow constant circulation. You want the steam to be able to escape.

Solar Drying

This is very popular and inexpensive, but the conditions have to be just right. To properly dehydrate food using the sun requires a minimum of three consecutive days of 95 degrees F temperature with extremely low humidity. This can be difficult to find depending on where you live. Also, not being able to control Mother Nature can prove difficult, too. So if this is feasible for your location, that's great; if not, there are other methods to try.

Food Dehydrator

Using a dehydrator costs very little and it is extremely efficient. It won't heat up the house, but if you're going to invest in one, go with one that has a temperature regulator so you can successfully dry a wider array of foods. Electric dehydration is more efficient than the oven. It works at low temperatures, which ensures the nutritional value of the food through the drying process. Simply follow the instructions manual for proper drying.

Dried Fruit and Fruit Leather

Even though it is relatively easy to find dried fruits and vegetables in the grocery stores, they are very expensive and often have preservatives that can be harmful. Besides, it's fun to be creative in the kitchen, especially if you're drying fruits and vegetables that you've grown yourself.

You can dry a wide variety of fruits, including apples, bananas, apricots, strawberries, blueberries, pears, peaches, and cherries. Dried fruits are generally leathery to crisp and may or may not be dipped in sugar or other seasonings to enhance flavors. You can also soak your fruits in flavored syrups if you'd like, although drying time may be significantly increased.

Here are a few initial basic steps:

- Pick fruit that is ripe but not overripe.

- Wash, pit, and slice fruit into uniform pieces to allow equal drying.

- If you want the color to stay intact, the fruit needs to be soaked in a mixture called a dip.

Dips prevent the loss of color in dried fruits. They also allow you to personalize your flavors. There are several different dips, but here are two favorites to get you started:

Honey Dip: This dip is good for tropical fruits such as bananas and pineapple. Simply mix together in a saucepan 1 cup of granulated sugar and 3 cups of water. Heat and stir until the sugar dissolves. Then add 1 cup of honey and stir until the honey is dissolved.

Ascorbic Acid Dip: This dip could be used for all fruit, but it works well with berries such as strawberries, blueberries, raspberries, etc. In a bowl, combine 5 crushed vitamin C tablets, 2 tablespoons of ascorbic acid, and ¼ cup of water. Stir until the vitamin C has dissolved.

Preparing your fruit is pretty simple, and the steps are specific to the fruit. Some of the most popular fruits to dry are apricots, peaches, apples, bananas, cherries, pears, strawberries, and blueberries. There are very few limitations as far as what you can dry.

Here are a few tips and caveats:

- For apricots, it works best to cut the fruit in half and turn inside out. They should be left to dry anywhere from 8 to 24 hours.

- Peaches need to be peeled and halved; they take 6 to 12 hours to dry.

- Apples need to be peeled and sliced into ¼-inch slices or rings; they take 6 to 12 hours to dry.

- Bananas have one of the most interesting flavors when dried. Peel them and slice into ¼-inch slices. Lay them flat on a sheet, and let them dry for 8 to 16 hours.

- Cherries need to be cut in half and dried for 18 to 26 hours, or until they get leathery (can take longer depending on the method and climate).

- Pears can be peeled and cut into ¼-inch slices. Dry for 6 to 20 hours.

- Strawberries need to be cut into ¼-inch slices, and they take approximately 6 to 16 hours to dry.

- Blueberries are simple; just lay them out on sheets and dry for 10 to 20 hours.

Fruit-Drying Methods

There are three ways to dry fruit: oven drying, solar drying, and electric dehydration. Drying does not necessarily mean applying heat to the fruit. Too much heat will draw the flavor and nutrition out of the fruit. When drying, the ideal temperature should stay between 120 and 140 degrees F. The fruit will take on a leathery appearance when fully dried.

- For **oven drying**, the temperature of the oven should be kept at less than 140 degrees F after the first hour. The last hour of drying is the most crucial. At this point, the fruit can easily burn and be ruined if the temperature is not closely monitored. Reduce temperatures dramatically during the last hour, and check on the fruit frequently for any signs of burning or overdrying. Feel free to taste a piece or two to check doneness. When the drying is completed, put the fruit in a pot or jar without a lid and leave in a dry, warm place for no longer than two weeks. Be sure to stir at least once a day.

- **Sun drying** is the most complicated method of the three but also the cheapest. It requires a climate with 95 to 100 degree F weather and low humidity. Other than that it's fairly easy. Spread the slices of fruit on a screen for three to four days, and turn once a day. Also, it is very important to bring them inside at night to keep moisture from returning to the fruit, which can allow bacteria and mold to grow. Store them in a dry area with good circulation until morning.

- For **dehydrators**, simply follow the manufacturer's instructions.

Prep Tip

A tool called a natural-draft dryer is a great way to simplify sun drying. It speeds the drying process by trapping heat from the sun, and it keeps the food from being infested by bugs or birds.

Storing Dried Fruits

If you want to store your dried fruits long term, the best way is in the freezer. Simply store in a resealable bag or freezer jar, making sure it is airtight.

Another great way to store fruit is by making fruit leather. Fruit leather is basically smashed and liquidized fruit that is heated at high temperatures until boiling and then spread thinly on a large sheet pan and cooled. Instead of buying commercial fruit leather for your kids, you can make your own without added sugars and preservatives. Kids will love the idea of eating fruit they've grown at home, too. The following are some basic starter recipes for making homemade fruit leather.

Fruit Leather Recipes

Basic Fruit Leather

Here is a basic recipe that you can easily use for whatever fruit you wish. These instructions are for oven drying; however, if you have a food dehydrator, it is a much easier process.

- Fresh fruit (peaches, plums, berries, apples, pears, grapes, etc.)
- Water
- Lemon juice
- Granulated sugar (if needed)
- Spices such as ground cinnamon and ground nutmeg (these are good with any fruit but are optional)

1. Preheat the oven to 150 degrees F (or 140 degrees if your oven has that setting).

2. When portioning fruit, keep in mind that 4 cups of fruit make approximately one sheet of leather.

3. Rinse and remove any pits, peels, cores, or stems. Always taste the fruit you are using. You may or may not need sugar. If it is sweet, then do not add any extra sweetness. If it is tart, like an apple, then add some sugar when instructed.

4. Place the fruit in a large saucepan. Add ½ cup of water for every 4 cups of chopped fruit. Bring to a simmer, cover, and let cook on a low heat until the fruit is fully cooked.

5. Uncover and stir. Use a potato masher to crush the fruit, or you can process the fruit in a food processor. Taste the fruit and decide whether to add sugar; also determine how much lemon juice or spices to add.

6. It is best to add sugar in small amounts (1 tablespoon at a time if working with 4 cups of fruit) to desired level of sweetness.

7. Add lemon juice 1 teaspoon at a time to help brighten the flavor of the fruit. Add a pinch or two of cinnamon, nutmeg, or other spices to allow the flavor to stand out.

8. Simmer and stir until all the sugar is dissolved and the fruit puree has thickened, usually about 5 to 10 minutes.

9. The puree should be very smooth.

10. Line a baking sheet with microwave-safe plastic wrap. Pour out the puree into the lined baking sheet to a thickness of either ⅛ inch or ¼ inch, depending on how thick you like it.

11. Place the baking sheet in the oven. Check that no plastic wrap is on top of the puree, or it will not dry out correctly.

12. Let the puree remain in the oven until it is dry and has formed a fruit leather. This usually takes 8 to 10 hours. The fruit leather is ready when it is not sticky and the surface is smooth.

13. When the fruit leather is ready, you can easily peel it from the plastic wrap.

14. To store it, simply roll it up in the plastic wrap, put it in an airtight container, and store in the refrigerator or freezer.

Apricot Leather

• 1 teaspoon fresh lemon juice	• 2 cups pitted and diced fresh apricots
	• ½ cup granulated sugar

1. Preheat the oven to 150 degrees F or the lowest setting available.

2. Combine the lemon juice, apricots, and sugar in a saucepan. Cook over medium heat until the sugar dissolves. Transfer to a blender or food processor, and puree until smooth.

3. Line an 11 x 17–inch pan or cookie sheet with a layer of microwaveable plastic wrap. Pour the pureed fruit onto the wrap and spread evenly, leaving 1 inch clear around the edges.

4. Bake for 4 to 6 hours, leaving the door slightly ajar, until the puree has dried and is no longer sticky.

5. Once dry, you can cut it into strips, wrap it in plastic wrap, and store in an airtight container.

Strawberry Leather

- 1 pound fresh strawberries, halved
- ¼ cup water
- 2 tablespoons granulated sugar (optional)
- 2 tablespoons honey

---

1. Preheat oven to 170 degrees F.

2. Place the strawberries and water in a saucepan, and bring to a boil. Cook for 3 minutes, until the berries start to soften.

3. Puree the berries with a blender or food processor. Return the puree to the saucepan, stir in the sugar, if needed, and the honey.

4. Cook for an additional 10 minutes or until thick and gooey.

5. Line an 11 x 17–inch pan or cookie sheet with a layer of microwaveable plastic wrap. Pour the pureed fruit onto the wrap and spread evenly, leaving 1 inch clear around the edges.

6. Place in the oven to dry for 3 hours. Turn off the oven and allow the leather to sit overnight, until completely dry.

7. Once dry, you can cut it into strips, wrap it in plastic wrap, and store in an airtight container.

Tropical Fruit Leather

- 4 cups fresh pineapple chunks
- 4 cups fresh mango, flesh only
- 1 cup fresh coconut flesh
- 4 whole bananas, peeled
- 1 cup water
- 2 tablespoons fresh lemon juice
- 2 tablespoons granulated sugar

1. Place all of the ingredients in a blender or food processor and puree. Put into a large saucepan and cook on medium heat until mixture comes to a slow simmer. Cook at a simmer until the sugar is completely dissolved and the fruit mixture starts to get thick, approximately 15 to 20 minutes.

2. Remove from the heat and allow to cool for a few minutes. Taste it to make sure that it's sweet enough and add a bit more sugar if you'd like.

3. Smear in a thin ⅛- to ¼-inch thick layer onto your dehydrator's fruit leather sheets (these can be purchased if your dehydrator didn't come with them).

4. Dehydrate at 140 degrees F for 6 to 8 hours. The leather will dry from the outside edges in and will be done when it holds its shape and peels off the plastic freely.

Spiced Apple Rings

- 15 medium apples
- 2 tablespoons lemon juice
- ½ cup granulated sugar
- 1 teaspoon ground cinnamon

- ½ teaspoon ground nutmeg
- ½ teaspoon ground allspice

---

1. Core the apples and slice them into ¼-inch-thick rings. Only peel the apples if you want to—they're perfectly delicious (and nutritious) with the peels.

2. Place the apples in a bowl of water with the lemon juice so they don't turn brown.

3. In a smaller bowl, combine the sugar and spices. Remove the apples from the water a few rings at a time and lay them on a paper towel. Blot dry and line in a single layer on a cookie sheet. Sprinkle with the sugar and spice mixture and flip over. Sprinkle the other side of the rings.

4. Place in a single layer on your dehydrator racks, and dehydrate for 4 to 6 hours at 135 degrees F or medium. They're done when they're leathery with no signs of moisture when you tear them.

Yields about ¾ pound.

Dried Sugared Pineapples

• 1 pineapple	• ½ cup granulated sugar

1. Core and peel the pineapple. Then slice it into ½-inch-thick rings. Finally, cut the rings into chunks.

2. Put the sugar in a small bowl, and toss the pineapple in it a few slices at a time.

3. Layer the pineapple in a single layer on your dehydrator racks, and dry for 24 to 36 hours at 135 degrees F or medium. These will still be sticky because of the high sugar content. For a healthier snack, skip the sugar.

Yields about 8 ounces.

Antioxidant Mix

- 2 cups pitted cherries
- 2 cups blueberries
- 2 cups sliced strawberries
- 2 cups blanched cranberries
- 2 cups apple pieces
- 2 tablespoons fresh lemon juice

1. Combine all of the fruits in a large bowl and drizzle the lemon juice over them. Toss to combine.

2. Layer in a single layer on the dehydrator racks, and dry at 140 degrees F for 24 to 36 hours or until chewy and leathery.

Yields about 2 cups.

Island Banana Chips

• 6 medium-ripe bananas	• 1 cup pineapple juice

1. Slice the bananas into ¼-inch slices, and place them immediately in the pineapple juice. Peel the bananas as you cut them. The citric acid in the juice will keep them from turning brown, and the juice will add a nice sweet flavor, too.

2. Layer the banana slices onto the dehydrator racks in a single layer, and dry at 140 degrees F (or medium) for 12 to 24 hours or until they're pliable with no visible sign of moisture. The longer you dry them, the crispier they will get.

Yields about 1 cup.

Drying Vegetables

Any vegetable that is going to be dried, with the exception of mushrooms, onions, and peppers, needs be washed, sliced, and blanched first. All the vegetables must be lined in a single layer on a cookie sheet or large tray to ensure even drying. All vegetables must be dried at 130 degrees F. If you dry them at too high or too low a temperature, the texture isn't going to be right and you may ruin the entire batch of produce.

The process of drying vegetables is almost identical to drying fruits, except that you probably won't use any sugar.

While you're learning to dehydrate foods, it's best to stick with common vegetables that are easily dried. Some of the best vegetables to start with include:

- Beets
- Broccoli
- Carrots
- Cauliflower
- Corn
- Green beans
- Mushrooms
- Onions
- Peas
- Potatoes
- Sweet peppers
- Tomatoes
- Zucchini

Now that you have a general list of veggies to start with, here are some quick and easy directions for drying these vegetables. Try them a few times, and experiment with flavors and spices. As long as you get them sufficiently dried, the worst thing that can happen is that you'll need to season them when you're cooking with them later.

- Beets are a bit messy, so wear gloves. Cook and peel beets, and cut into slices or ¼-inch pieces. They take 3 to 10 hours to dry completely, and they should be slightly leathery.

- Before drying green beans, wash them in cold water and break all the stems off. Break beans into approximately 1-inch pieces. Then they need to be blanched. Afterward, dry for about 6 to 12 hours. They should be brittle.

- Carrots are great to dry, but they get pretty tough. You can either shred them or slice them. Before cutting, wash carrots in cold water and then peel. Dry for 6 to 12 hours, until almost brittle.

- After washing cauliflower, cut into uniform florets, and dry for 6 to 14 hours.

- Corn is probably one of the most time-consuming to dry. First the corn must be dehusked and cleaned, blanched, and then cut off the cob. Try not to get any of the cob into the cuttings. Lay the corn out evenly on a tray or sheet and dry for 6 to 12 hours.

- Broccoli is very similar to cauliflower: wash, cut into florets, and then dry for 4 to 10 hours.

- Onions are very widely used in cooking and are extremely good to have on hand. They also take up lots of space, so drying them is a really efficient way to save space. Slice them about ¼ inch thick, and dry for 6 to 12 hours. They will be crisp when done.

- Mushrooms should not be cleaned with water—simply wipe off any dirt and then either slice or leave them whole, depending on the type of mushroom. The drying time is a bit different as well because mushrooms are sensitive to heat. They need to be dried at a temperature of 90 degrees F for 3 hours, and 125 degrees F for the rest of the drying time. Mushrooms have a total drying time of approximately 4 to 10 hours, until they are brittle.

- Peas are super easy. Blanch slightly, pour onto tray, and dry for 5 to 12 hours. Peas are great when added to a rice-cracker mix or trail mix.

- With a bit of salt, potatoes make a great dried snack. Slice the potatoes into extra-thin slices, and dry for 6 to 12 hours until crisp like a potato chip.

- Zucchini makes a tasty chip as well. Wash, slice thin, and dry for 5 to 10 hours. These should be brittle.

- Tomatoes are a bit more work. Dunk each tomato in boiling water; this will make the skin fall off easier. Peel and either quarter or slice. Dry for 6 to 12 hours until they are nice and crisp.

- Sweet peppers are delicious dried and having them pre-prepped for a meal is a huge time-saver. Remove all the seeds, and chop or leave whole (depends on the size of the pepper). They take about 5 to 12 hours to become leathery.

Dried Veggie Recipes

Dried Trinity

This is a staple in nearly all soups and bases. Having a supply in an emergency situation can bring flavor and nutrition to meats, stews, and even rice and pasta.

- 3 cups chopped celery
- 3 cups chopped carrots
- 3 cups chopped onions
- 2 teaspoons salt (optional)

---

1. Mix the celery, carrots, onions, and salt together in a big bowl.

2. Spread in the dehydrator in a single layer. Dry at 140 degrees F for 4 to 6 hours or until the veggies are crispy. Test for doneness by placing in a sealed baggie or jar for 24 hours and watching for condensation. If there is none, dry can or vacuum seal to increase shelf life. Dry canning and vacuum packing is explained in the next chapter.

Yields about 1 cup.

Pepper Fiesta

- 3 cups rough chopped red bell peppers
- 3 cups rough chopped green bell peppers
- 1 cup rough chopped chile or jalapeño peppers, seeded if you want to remove the heat
- 2 tablespoons fresh lemon juice
- 1 tablespoon salt

1. Combine all the peppers in a large mixing bowl, and toss with the lemon juice and salt.

2. Spread mixture on your dehydrator trays in single layers. Dry at 140 degrees F for 3 to 5 hours or until the peppers are crunchy crisp.

Yields about 1 cup.

Candied Zucchini Cubes

This may sound a bit odd, but these are actually delicious as well as nutritious. They're great in zucchini bread or even cupcakes or muffins. Add them to your yogurt, or dry can or vacuum seal it for survival stash.

- 1 cup brown sugar
- 1 cup granulated sugar
- 1½ cups water
- 1½ tablespoons fresh lemon juice
- 8 medium zucchini, peeled and cubed into ½-inch cubes

1. Bring the sugars, water, and lemon juice to a simmer with a large saucepan until the sugars are dissolved. Add the zucchini and simmer for about 5 minutes, until it starts to become soft. Remove from the heat and place in a glass container. Refrigerate overnight.

2. Drain the zucchini cubes and pat dry. Layer them in a single layer with breathing room on the dehydrator trays. Dehydrate at 130 degrees F for 8 to 10 hours or until there's no moisture left and they're rubbery. The cubes will firm up as they cool.

3. Do the bag or jar test to make sure that they're completely dehydrated before dry canning or vacuum sealing.

Yields about 1½ cups.

Home-Dried Fresh Herbs

Dried herbs and spices are a great way to help you avoid food fatigue in an emergency situation. With just a handful of basic herbs, you can make dozens of different flavor profiles. When you combine that with different cooking methods, your diet will remain diverse, nutritious, and creative with just a few different ingredients.

Quality herbs in the store are atrociously expensive and rarely as rewarding as using fresh herbs. Plus, drying your own homegrown herbs is very easy and a great way to preserve your herbs if you're not planning to grow them year round. They also make a great homestead gift.

Drying herbs is a slightly different process than for fruits and vegetables, but not by much. Mainly the cooking temperature and times change. You can use any of the three drying techniques mentioned earlier to dry herbs, too, but oftentimes, applying any heat to the herbs tends to rob them of their natural oils, which in turn, diminishes the flavor.

Air-drying herbs is not only the easiest and least-expensive way to dry fresh herbs, but this slow-drying process also doesn't leach the herbs of their oils. This process works best with dryer herbs like bay leaf, dill, marjoram, oregano, rosemary, savory, and thyme. Moisture-rich herbs such as basil, chives, mint, and tarragon fare better in a dehydrator or by freezing.

If you are harvesting the herbs from your own garden, here are some tips:

- Pick them before flowering occurs (if you pick them often, flowering won't occur).

- Picking is best done in the morning after the dew has dried, but before the sun wilts the herbs.

- Cut hydrated, healthy-looking branches from your herb plants. Remove any dry or possibly diseased leaves.

- Shake to remove any bugs.

- If necessary, rinse with cold water and dry with paper towels. Make sure to dry them well because wet herbs will mold and rot.

- Remove the lower leaves along the very bottom of the branch. Group four to six branches together and tie them with a rubber band. The groups will shrink as they dry, so they need to be tightened throughout the drying process or you will end up with a mess on the floor. Small groups are best for herbs with high moisture content.

- Punch or cut several holes in a paper bag, and label the bag with the name of the herb you are drying. Put the correct herb group upside down into the bag.

- Wrap the ends of the bag around the bundle, and tie it closed. Make sure the herbs are not too cramped inside the bag.

- Hang the bag upside down in a warm, well-circulated room.

Check in after about two weeks to see how things are progressing, but do not forget to tighten the bands every so often. After the initial check-in, keep checking weekly until the herbs are dry and ready to store.

Here are some tips on storing the dried herbs:

- Use small jars (baby food jars work great)

- Freeze them in a resealable bag or freezer jar with an airtight seal.

- Leaves are best left whole; crush when you are ready to use (for better flavor preservation).

- Keep a close eye, and discard any moldy leaves.

- Store the herbs in a dry, dark place away from sunlight.

- Use within a year for best results.

- A teaspoon of dried herbs is equal to a tablespoon of fresh herbs.

Medicinal Herbs

Although it's outside the scope of this particular book, many different herbs can be used for healing and preventive medicine. Some are easy to grow and dry and may make the difference between life and death in a survival situation.

Even though you'll need to collect a stockpile of any life-sustaining medications that you or a family member needs, there's never a guarantee that something catastrophic won't happen to eliminate your ability to obtain more. In preparation for that, you may want to learn about alternative natural treatments for any conditions that you may have. Maybe that sounds alarmist, but it never hurts to be prepared.

You can find many interesting and easy-to-read books on medicinal herbs on the Internet or at your local bookstore, and it's recommended that you pick one of these up in paperback so that you have it in your bug-out bag or emergency kit.

Drying Meats

Three factors have caused a sharp increase in home-drying meat in recent years. First and foremost, more and more people have become conscious of what's in commercially prepared foods. They're typically high in sodium, dyes, and chemical preservatives, making them nonviable as a healthy protein source. Rising grocery costs are another factor, and finally, people are beginning to worry about storing food for emergency situations.

Dehydrating meat is a wonderful way to preserve a nutritious, delicious, and portable source of quality protein. There are some guidelines that you need to follow, however, to dehydrate your meat safely:

Prepper's Checklist   Dehydrating Safety

- ☐ Wash your hands thoroughly before starting and after handling the meat.
- ☐ Keep meat refrigerated until it's time to dry it.
- ☐ Thaw frozen meat in the fridge. Don't use frozen meat in the dehydrator.
- ☐ Slice meat uniformly.
- ☐ Marinate meat in the fridge, not on the counter.
- ☐ Never reuse marinade.
- ☐ Don't marinate more meat than you can dehydrate in a 24-hour period.
- ☐ Don't mix poultry, fish, or red meats while marinating. Keep them all separate.
- ☐ Use lean meat with little to no visible fat. Fat goes rancid faster than protein.

Preparing Your Meat for Dehydrating

As with any food product, there are pathogens present in meat that can be harmful or even lethal if consumed. The big ones you have to worry about in meat products include *Escherichia coli*, *Listeria monocytogenes*, *Salmonella*, and *Staphylococcus aureus*. If you've ever suffered from food poisoning, you know that even a mild dose of these pathogens is extremely unpleasant, to say the least. At worst, it can kill you, so make sure that you follow safety guidelines above carefully when drying meat.

Basically, use your head. Many of these tips are simple common sense, and you can greatly increase the safety of drying your meat just by observing standard food handling safety practices.

Drying Your Meat

This is the important part: if you don't dry your meat at the proper temperature for the right amount of time, it's not going to be properly preserved. As already discussed, you run the risk of foodborne pathogens, but it may also simply mold if you don't dry it long enough, or become tasteless and brittle if you dry it for too long. Here are some tips:

- Use a dehydrator with a temperature setting, and dry your meat at 140 degrees F for the recommended time.

- To visually test for doneness, bend the meat. If you can see moisture glistening inside it, it isn't done.

- Dry the meat to an internal temperature of 160 degrees F. To test a batch, create one piece of "test" meat that's a little thicker than the rest. Once that piece reaches that temperature, then the others will have as well.

Prep Tip

Dry canning or vacuum sealing jerky will further preserve dried meats. See the next section for more information.

Dried-Meat Recipes

Beef Jerky

Although called "beef" jerky, it's great with any type of lean red meat that you'd like to use. Venison is a great substitute because it's lean and extremely nutritious.

- 16 ounces soy sauce
- 16 ounces Worcestershire sauce
- 2 teaspoons garlic powder
- 2 teaspoons onion powder
- 1 teaspoon freshly ground black pepper
- 1 teaspoon cayenne pepper (optional)
- 1 teaspoon red pepper flakes (optional)
- 4 pounds lean beef, thinly sliced with the grain

1. Mix the sauces and spices together in a large bowl, and add the meat, mixing so that each piece is coated.

2. Refrigerate for 12 to 24 hours, stirring every couple of hours.

3. Dry for 10 to 12 hours or according to your dehydrator's instructions. The meat is dry when it bends with no visible moisture.

Yields about 1 pound of jerky.

Chicken Jerky

Be extremely careful working with raw chicken, because poultry is notoriously dangerous when it comes to pathogens. You can use turkey breast for this if you prefer.

- 16 ounces soy sauce
- 3 teaspoons lemon juice
- 2 teaspoons cracked black pepper
- 2 teaspoons powdered garlic
- 1 teaspoon ground ginger
- 1 teaspoon onion powder
- 4 pounds boneless, skinless chicken breast, trimmed and sliced with the grain ¼-inch thick

1. Mix all the ingredients except the chicken in a large bowl, and add the meat, mixing so that each piece is coated.

2. Marinate the chicken for 12 to 24 hours, stirring occasionally.

3. Dry in a single layer per tray at 145 degrees F for 6 to 8 hours, depending upon your dehydrator and how thick your strips are.

Yields about 1 pound of jerky.

Packaging and Storing Dehydrated Meat

The best way to preserve your meat for long-term storage is to dry-can it or vacuum-pack it. Otherwise, it's good for only a couple of weeks after dehydration. Before you do either though, there's a moisture test that you need to conduct to make sure that the meat is dry enough. Place a few strips in a jar or in a sealed bag, and let them sit for a few hours, up to 24 hours. If there is condensation in the bag, the meat isn't dry enough and you need to put it back in the dehydrator.

If you're going to eat the meat within a couple of weeks, you can store it at room temperature in a sealed container for up to 2 weeks as long as it's properly dried. If you'd like to make it part of your emergency food supply, however, you need to either dry-can it or vacuum-pack it to keep it for longer than a couple of weeks. The next chapter has more on dry canning and vacuuming packing.

13

STORING YOUR DRIED AND CANNED FOODS

You've worked hard to can or dry your food, and it would be a shame to waste all of that effort by not storing your foods in a manner conducive to extending their shelf life. Three factors play a huge role in how well your foods will stand the test of time: temperature, temperature fluctuation, and humidity. If you've dried or preserved your foods properly, humidity shouldn't be much of an issue, but that still leaves temperature.

There's a reason why cellars are often underground or built into the side of a hill: those places maintain a constant, cool temperature that's conducive to extending the shelf life of practically all foods. As a matter of fact, the U.S. Food and Drug Administration (FDA) states that when storing seeds, each 10 degrees of temperature drop doubles the shelf life of seeds. This applies to food, too, at least to a certain degree.

Temperature fluctuation has a huge effect, too. Foods that are warmed and cooled several times will change color and even flavor and texture. Nutritional value is lost, too, and if it becomes warm enough to affect the seals on canned goods, you may lose your food to spoilage. Since light alters temperature, it's best to make sure that your storage place is dark.

To put it in a nutshell, store your foods in a cool, dark place that doesn't have temperature fluctuations if you want to get the longest shelf life possible. It's still important to rotate your emergency food supply, too.

There are a couple of additional things that you can do to preserve your hard work. Dehydrated foods are great, but as mentioned previously, they still have a limited shelf life. To preserve them for much longer periods, you can opt to dry-can them or vacuum-pack them.

Dry-Canning

Dry-canning is super simple and requires only an oven. It's a great way to preserve dry goods for even longer than what the original shelf life is. As a matter of fact, when dry-canned properly, goods can last for as long as 20 years. This is a great way to save a lot of money when building your emergency food supply, because you can buy in bulk and can your goods in portions that won't go bad. It also makes sharing and bartering easier in survivalist situations. Just a few foods that can be dry-canned include:

- Jerky
- Dried fruits and veggies
- Flour
- Rice
- Potato flakes
- Cake mixes
- Cornmeal
- Any other dry food with a low moisture content

Dry-canning kills any bugs or eggs that may be in the flour and seals the product so that it's impervious to any kind of infestation or even damage caused by exposure to moisture or humid conditions. All that you need are your jars, seals, bands, and an oven.

High-fat foods such as nuts can't be dry-canned, because the fat goes rancid. If you're dry-canning dehydrated foods, make sure they're properly dried to eliminate as much moisture as possible from the product.

Steps to Dry-Canning

This is an extremely simple process. Follow your jar-prepping procedures by making sure that your jars are sterile, but make sure that for this process they're also dry. Moisture in the jar can be absorbed by the dry product and cause spoilage. Follow these easy steps to ensure success.

1.	Preheat oven to 200 degrees F.
2.	Pack dry goods, jerky, or dried produce into canning jars.
3.	Put a cookie sheet in the oven to set the jars on.
4.	Put open jars full of food in the oven on the cookie sheet.
5.	Leave in the oven for 1 hour.
6.	Carefully remove 1 jar at a time from the oven.
7.	Wipe the rims to remove any oil or debris.
8.	Center the lids on each jar, and screw the band on fingertight.
9.	Allow to cool. Jars will seal as they cool.
10.	Date each jar, and label with its contents.
11.	Store the jars in a cool, dry place until ready for use.

Now you know how to dry-can and have yet another food storage option to help you quickly build an emergency food supply.

Dry-Canned Butter

Dry-canning butter is a simple process and will be something that you'll really thank yourself for in an emergency situation. Not only will it be a great cooking ingredient, but also it will be good for bartering because it's a luxury item that most people won't think to stock. Use full-fat, good-quality butter; this is one of those times that it just won't do to cut corners. If you can get fresh organic butter, that's even better. Storing in half-pint jars may be best if there are just a few people in your family, because it will begin to go rancid quickly without refrigeration.

- Full-fat butter, salted or unsalted
- Half-pint jars, lids, and bands

---

1. Heat your jars in the oven at 250 degrees F for 20 minutes. Meanwhile, prepare lids and bands by simmering them over low heat in a small saucepan.

2. Melt the butter over low to medium heat. Each half-pint will hold about ½ pound of butter.

3. Pour the butter into the jars using a funnel and perhaps a ladle.

4. Remove air bubbles, wipe rims, center the lids, and screw on the bands and adjust until they are fingertip tight.

5. Add the lids and bands. Tighten fingertip tight. Jars will seal as the butter cools. When jars are room temperature, put in the fridge or someplace cool so that the butter solidifies, and then store in a cool, dry place out of the sunlight. As long as it seals, it will be good for up to 3 years.

Yields ½ pound of butter per half-pint jar.

Vacuum-Packing

The enemies of dried foods are moisture and air. The previous section discussed how valuable dry-canning can be to combat moisture and air, but what if you need to leave in a hurry or don't have a lot of space for storing food? You may want to consider vacuum-packing. You'll need a vacuum-packing machine and bags. Here are some tips to get you started:

- If a food needs refrigeration prior to vacuum-packing, it's going to need refrigeration afterward as well.

- Before you vacuum-pack your dried foods, do the moisture test on them: Place them in a jar with a lid or in a resealable bag for a few hours. If there's condensation, the food isn't dry enough and should be dehydrated some more. Spoilage is still an issue.

- Foods high in oil such as nuts will still go rancid even if you vacuum-pack them.

- Vacuum-pack single servings or daily servings only. Once they're open, the spoilage clock is ticking.

- Make sure that all the air that you can possibly get out of the bag is out.

Vacuum-packing food is a fairly simple process but will vary slightly depending upon your vacuum-packing machine and bags. In general, however, all that you'll need to do is put the food in the bag and seal it according to the manufacturer's instructions. Date it and store in a cool, dry place until you're ready to use. Remember to rotate your stock and follow storage directions.

One final point that is important to maintaining a good emergency food supply is proper rotation. To ensure that the older foods are being eaten first, date everything and place the newest food in the rear of your supply. That way, all you have to do when you access your stored foods is take the product that's in front. And it's one more way to make sure that your hard work isn't wasted. After all, even food that you prepare yourself isn't cheap, and wasting is an expensive proposition.

Quick and Easy Prepper Recipes

We've discussed how to can foods in boiling water baths and in pressure canners. We've talked about dehydrators and dry canning and even touched on vacuum packing. But what about when you're really in an emergency situation? Hopefully, you've stored your foodstuffs and heating methods so you can continue to prepare hot meals.

To make outdoor cooking infinitely easier, you really should consider investing in at least one medium-sized Dutch oven, a fire rack, and a set of iron skillets in different sizes. If you have the extra resources, a kettle with a tripod is great. Remember that food isn't just about survival; it's also about morale and keeping spirits up. You can still eat good meals even in stark circumstances . . . as long as you prepare.

Since cooking on an open fire is the most common way to cook without power, this is the method used for most of the following recipes. Most of them transfer very well to traditional cooking, too, so don't feel like you have to wait. They're delicious!

Breads

Bread is a staple survival food; it helps fill you up and provides valuable carbs for energy. All of these breads can be baked or fried, and you can also add herbs, seasonings, or chopped fruits or vegetables to them if you'd like.

Basic Piecrust

This can be used for anything from desserts to potpies and is a quick, easy source of flavor, fat, and carbs. Use your canned butter (see the chapter on dry canning) and dry goods.

- 2 cups all-purpose flour
- ¼ teaspoon salt
- ⅔ cup butter, chilled if possible
- 4–5 tablespoons cold water

1. Combine the flour and salt in a bowl, and then cut in the butter until it is spread throughout the flour in pea-sized chunks.

2. Add 4 tablespoons of the water and combine gently. If it's too dry to hold a ball shape, add the other tablespoon of water until the pie dough forms without being sticky. If it gets too sticky, just add a sprinkle of flour.

3. Separate into two balls. When ready to use it, lightly flour a surface and roll 1 dough ball out with a glass, a bottle, or a rolling pin, if you have one, to desired thickness. Use immediately.

Yields 2 piecrusts.

Simple Bread

It's not fancy, but it will do.

- 2 cups all-purpose flour
- 1 teaspoon salt
- 3 tablespoons baking powder
- 2 tablespoons shortening or butter
- About ½ cup water or canned milk
- Oil for skillet

---

1. Mix the flour, salt, and baking powder together in a bowl, and cut in the shortening until it resembles pea-sized crumble.

2. Add the liquid a little at a time until the dough is kneadable but not sticky.

3. Lightly oil an iron skillet and heat over medium fire. Drop the dough into the skillet, and fry on each side until brown.

Yields about 4.

Johnnycakes

- 2 cups cornmeal
- 2 eggs or the equivalent in reconstituted powdered eggs
- ¾ cup water
- 2 tablespoons granulated sugar
- ½ teaspoon salt
- Oil for skillet

---

1. Mix all the ingredients together in a bowl, and heat a greased skillet over medium fire. Your batter should be thin but not runny—similar to pancake batter. If it's too thin, add a bit more cornmeal. If it's too thick, add a little more water.

2. Pour by the quarter cup into the skillet, and fry for about 2 minutes or until the cake starts to look dry on top and is brown on the bottom. Flip and fry for 1 minute or until bottom is brown. Remove from the fire and eat.

3. These will store for a few days without refrigeration if you seal them up to keep them from drying out.

Yields about 6 cakes.

Survival Bread

If you use gelatin, this loaf of bread has all of the macronutrients that one adult needs in a day. It's lacking in vitamins and minerals, however, so you can survive on it temporarily, but you won't thrive long-term.

- 2 tablespoons water
- 3 tablespoons honey
- 1 package lemon gelatin (optional; also try orange and lime)
- 2 cups old-fashioned oats
- 1 cup granulated sugar
- 2¼ cups fresh milk or reconstituted powdered milk

1. Put the water and honey in a saucepan, and add gelatin, if you're using it. Heat over medium fire until dissolved. Remove from the heat, and add the oats, sugar, and milk to the liquid. If the mixture is too dry to shape, add more water a few drops at a time. If it's too wet, add a little more oatmeal.

2. Shape into a flat loaf or a few individual bars, and bake in a skillet over medium fire for 15–20 minutes. Allow to cool, and store in foil or a resealable bag.

Yields 5 servings.

Survivalist Cornbread

For the milk and eggs, you can use reconstituted powder or the real thing, depending upon what you have.

- 2 cups white or yellow cornmeal
- 2 cups all-purpose flour
- 1 cup granulated sugar
- 2 teaspoons salt
- 2 tablespoons baking powder
- 2 eggs or the equivalent of reconstituted powdered eggs
- 2 cups fresh milk or reconstituted powdered milk
- 2/3 cup melted butter or oil
- 1 can creamed corn (optional)
- 2 tablespoons pickled or fresh jalapeño, sliced (optional)

1. Preheat a Dutch oven over medium fire.

2. Combine all the dry ingredients in a bowl, then add the remaining ingredients and stir until combined. The batter may be slightly lumpy.

3. Pour into the hot Dutch oven and cover. Bake for 20 minutes over medium fire or until brown and a knife inserted in the center comes out clean.

Yields about 9 servings or 18 slices.

Sweet Flatbread

- 2 cups all-purpose flour
- ¼ teaspoon salt
- ⅔ cup water
- 1 tablespoon butter, melted
- ¼ cup granulated sugar
- 1 tablespoon ground cinnamon
- Oil for skillet

1. Combine the flour and salt in a bowl. Add the water and butter, and stir until combined.

2. Turn out on a floured surface and knead until a malleable dough forms. Divide into 2-inch balls.

3. Roll a ball out into a strip, and sprinkle with sugar and cinnamon. Fold it onto itself, and roll again until it's a thin strip.

4. Place in a hot greased skillet, and fry for 30 seconds on each side, or until brown.

5. Repeat steps 3 and 4 until all the balls are fried.

Yields about 10 pieces.

Herbed Flatbread

- 2 cups all-purpose flour
- 1 teaspoon salt
- 1 tablespoon dried basil
- 1 tablespoon dried rosemary
- 2 tablespoons oil or melted butter
- 2/3 cup water
- Oil for skillet

1. Mix the flour, salt, and herbs in a bowl. Add the oil or butter, and mix until there are pea-sized crumbles. Then add the water and stir.

2. Turn out onto a floured surface and knead until dough is smooth and elastic. Allow to rise for 45 minutes or so.

3. Divide into 2-inch balls and roll out flat.

4. Fry in a hot, greased skillet until browned on both sides.

Yields about 10 pieces.

Indian Fry Bread

- 3 cups all-purpose flour
- 1 teaspoon salt
- 1½ tablespoons baking powder
- 2 cups warm (not hot) water
- Oil for skillet

1. Mix the dry ingredients in a bowl, then add the warm water ½ cup at a time until a dough is formed. Knead the mixture until it's not sticky, adding a bit more flour if necessary.

2. Divide into 2-inch balls. Roll out each ball as thin as possible, and fry on a hot, greased griddle or iron skillet. Brown on both sides.

Yields about 10 slices.

Dutch Oven Biscuits

- 4 cups all-purpose flour
- 1 teaspoon salt
- 2 tablespoons baking powder
- ½ cup shortening or lard
- 1½ cups buttermilk, water, fresh milk, or reconstituted powdered milk
- Oil for Dutch oven

1. Heat a Dutch oven over medium fire.

2. Mix together the dry ingredients in a bowl, then cut in the shortening until the mixture is crumbly. Add the liquid and stir just until mixed. Don't overstir, or the biscuits will be tough.

3. If you'd like, you can roll them out on a floured surface and cut them, or you can just drop the dough in uniform chunks into the greased Dutch oven.

4. Bake for 15–20 minutes with the lid on or until the biscuits are browned.

Yields about 8–10 biscuits.

Raisin Flatbread

Surviving a disaster, especially a long-term one, depends largely on morale. Sometimes you need a bit of a treat, and this easy-to-make bread fits the bill.

- 2 cups all-purpose flour
- 2 tablespoons baking powder
- 2 tablespoons granulated sugar
- 2 tablespoons raisins
- 1 tablespoon ground cinnamon
- 2 pinches salt
- ½ cup warm water
- Oil for skillet

1. Mix the dry ingredients together in a bowl, and add in just enough warm water to make the dough manageable.

2. Pat the dough out into a loaf and fry it in a greased iron skillet. The dough will get brown and crisp.

Yields 1 loaf.

Breakfast Foods and Desserts

Breakfast is arguably the most important meal of the day, especially in a situation where you're burning calories rapidly. These recipes are simple to make, delicious, and nutritious. When prepping for a disaster situation, be sure to stock coffee, powdered milk, powdered eggs, and plenty of dried goods.

Campfire Coffee

Chances are good that you're not going to have your electric espresso maker, so here's a great way to make a pot of coffee in a pan.

- 1 teaspoon ground coffee
- Coffee filter
- Needle and thread
- 8 ounces of water
- Pinch of salt

1. Spoon the coffee in a filter, fold the filter in half, and run a needle and thread around the edges of the filter, sewing it together. Pull the string tight and tie it so that the filter becomes a coffee pouch.

2. Combine the water and salt in a saucepan and bring it to a boil. Drop the pouch in. Boil for 5 minutes, give or take 1 minute, depending on how strong you want your coffee.

Yields 1 cup.

All-in-One Breakfast Scramble

- Oil for skillet
- 1 pound sausage, crumbled (canned sausage also works well)
- 6 fresh or canned potatoes, cubed
- 12 eggs or the equivalent of reconstituted powdered eggs
- 1 teaspoon salt
- ½ teaspoon black pepper
- Any veggies you'd like, such as peppers, onions, etc.

1. Heat a Dutch oven or large greased iron skillet over medium fire. Add the sausage and cook until browned, then add the potatoes.

2. When the sausage is done, beat the eggs and add them to the sausage and potatoes. Toss in the salt and pepper, along with any vegetables. Cook, stirring every couple of minutes, until done.

Yields 6 servings.

Campfire Muffins

This is just a base recipe. You can make it just like it is, or feel free to add orange peel, bananas, blueberries, nuts, or anything else that you'd like to have in them.

- 2 cups all-purpose flour
- ½ cup granulated sugar
- ½ teaspoon salt
- 1 tablespoon baking powder
- 1 cup fresh milk or reconstituted powdered milk
- 2 eggs or the equivalent of reconstituted powdered eggs
- ¼ cup butter, melted
- ½ cup berries, fruits, nuts, or whatever else you want (optional)

1. Preheat a Dutch oven over medium fire.

2. Combine all the dry ingredients, then add the milk, eggs, and butter. Stir until moist, but don't overstir, or your muffins will be tough. Add the fruit or other optional items, and fold into the batter.

3. Pour the batter into the Dutch oven, and cook covered for 15–20 minutes or until brown and a knife inserted in the center comes out clean.

4. Remove the Dutch oven from the heat. Allow to cool uncovered, then slice it into squares.

Yields about 8 servings.

Mixed Berry Crisp

- 4 cups canned or fresh berries
- ½ cup granulated sugar
- ½ cup all-purpose flour
- ½ cup rolled oats
- ½ cup packed brown sugar
- ½ cup butter, softened

1. Preheat a Dutch oven over medium fire.

2. Combine the fruit and sugar in a medium bowl.

3. In a separate bowl, combine the flour, oats, brown sugar, and butter until a crumble forms.

4. Mix fruit and sugar into the crumble, and spread in the bottom of a Dutch oven. Bake covered for 25 minutes or until the crumble is brown and the fruit is bubbly.

Yields about 6 servings.

Peach Cobbler

- 4 cups fresh or canned peaches
- ½ cup granulated sugar
- 1 teaspoon ground cinnamon
- ½ teaspoon ground allspice
- 2 cups self-rising flour
- ¾ cup fresh milk or reconstituted powdered milk
- ½ teaspoon salt

1. Preheat a Dutch oven over medium fire.

2. Combine the peaches, sugar, cinnamon, and allspice in a medium bowl, and set aside.

3. In a separate bowl, mix together the flour, milk, and salt. It should be similar to the consistency of pancake batter. If not, add a bit more flour or milk as needed.

4. Put the peaches in a Dutch oven and drizzle the flour batter over it. Bake covered for 25–30 minutes or until the batter is golden brown on top.

Yields about 6 servings.

Campfire Blueberry Flapjacks

- 2 cups all-purpose flour
- 1 teaspoon salt
- 1½ teaspoons baking soda
- 2 eggs or equivalent of reconstituted powdered eggs
- 1 tablespoon oil

- 1 cup milk, buttermilk, or reconstituted powdered milk
- ½ cup blueberries, fresh, canned, or reconstituted dried
- Oil for skillet

---

1. Combine the flour, salt, and baking soda in a medium bowl. Then mix in the eggs and oil. Stir just until combined; if you overstir, the flapjacks will be tough. Fold in the blueberries.

2. Pour by the quarter cup onto a hot, greased iron skillet or griddle over medium fire. Fry until the top is beginning to look dry and then flip, about 2 minutes. Brown the second side and remove from the heat. Repeat until the batter is gone.

Yields about 10 flapjacks.

Potato Cakes

- 2 cups leftover mashed potatoes, regular or instant
- 3 eggs or the equivalent of reconstituted powdered eggs
- ½ cup all-purpose flour
- ½ teaspoon salt
- Oil for skillet

---

1. Combine all the ingredients in a bowl.

2. Drop the mixture by quarter cups onto a hot greased skillet over medium fire. Brown on one side, about 2 minutes, and then flip and brown on the other side.

3. Serve with maple syrup or your choice of jam or jelly.

Yields about 6 cakes.

Campsite Hash Browns

- 2 cups fresh or canned shredded potatoes
- ½ cup onion
- 1 teaspoon salt
- 1 teaspoon black pepper
- ½ teaspoon dried rosemary (optional)
- Oil for skillet

1. Mix all the ingredients together in a bowl, and preheat a greased iron skillet over medium fire.

2. Fry until brown and crispy, stirring occasionally, about 20 minutes.

Yields 4 servings.

Apple Fritters

Fritters

- 2 cups all-purpose flour
- 1 tablespoon baking powder
- ½ teaspoon salt
- ½ cup granulated sugar
- 1 teaspoon ground allspice
- 2 eggs or the equivalent of reconstituted powdered eggs
- 1½ cups fresh milk or reconstituted powdered milk
- 1 cup oil or lard

Glaze

- 1 cup powdered sugar
- 1 teaspoon ground cinnamon
- 3 tablespoons fresh milk or reconstituted powdered milk
- 1 teaspoon orange zest (optional)

Fritters:

1. Combine the flour, baking powder, salt, sugar, and allspice in a bowl.

2. Add the eggs and milk, and stir until combined.

3. Preheat the oil in an iron skillet, and drop the batter by tablespoons into the oil. Fry until brown, turning as necessary. Remove from grease and drain on a towel.

Glaze:

1. Mix all the ingredients in a small bowl. Drizzle over the fritters and enjoy.

Yields about 15 fritters.

Cinnamon-Orange Raisin Rice

This is great to have premixed in a resealable bag for portability.

- ½ cup water
- ½ cup dry, instant rice
- 1 tablespoon raisins or dried cranberries
- 1 tablespoon dried, chopped, candied orange rinds
- 1 tablespoon powdered milk
- 2 teaspoons brown sugar or maple syrup

1. Bring water to a boil.

2. Combine the rest of the ingredients in a heatproof bowl, and pour the boiling water over it.

3. Let stand for a few minutes, until the rice is tender.

Yields 1 serving.

Strawberry-Almond Trail Mix

This is another great recipe to add to your bug-out bag. Just add water when on the trail. In a pinch, you can even eat it dry.

- ½ cup water
- 1 cup quick oats
- 2 tablespoons dried strawberries
- 2 tablespoons almonds
- 1 tablespoon brown sugar

1. Bring the water to a boil.

2. Combine the dry ingredients in a heatproof bowl or cup. Pour the boiling water over it, and stir until the oatmeal is wet.

3. Let steep for 1 minute until oats are soft, and enjoy.

Yields 1 serving.

Coffee Can Spam and Eggs

A coffee can is a great emergency cooking vessel. You can make everything from coffee to soup and bread in it.

- 3 eggs or the equivalent of reconstituted powdered eggs
- ½ cup Spam, cubed
- ½ cup fresh or canned potatoes, cubed
- 2 pinches salt
- 2 pinches black pepper

1. Crack the eggs into the coffee can, and whisk with a spoon. Add the spam, potatoes, salt, and pepper.

2. Place on the cooking rack or right in the outside ashes of the fire. Cook for 3 to 4 minutes, stirring occasionally.

3. Remove from the fire and transfer to a plate, or let the can cool for a couple of minutes and eat it right out of the can.

Yields 1 serving.

Mountain Man Sausage Gravy

- 1 quart canned breakfast sausage or 1 pound fresh sausage
- ½ cup all-purpose flour
- 2 cups water
- ½ cup canned milk (optional, if you don't have milk, just add more water)
- Salt and black pepper to taste

---

1. Fry the sausage in an iron skillet, and then sprinkle the flour over it, stirring until the flour coats the sausage and browns. Be careful not to let it burn, because the gravy will taste singed.

2. Slowly add the water, ½ cup at a time, stirring vigorously and constantly to avoid lumps. Add the milk last, if you choose to use it. Taste and add salt and pepper as necessary.

3. Serve over Dutch Oven Biscuits (recipe provided earlier) or scrambled eggs.

Yields about 4 cups.

Corned Beef Hash

- 1 (15-ounce) can corned beef
- Oil for skillet
- 1½ cups fresh or canned diced potatoes
- ½ cup diced onion
- Salt and black pepper to taste

1. Add the corned beef to a preheated greased skillet over medium fire, using a wooden spoon to break it up into crumbles. Add the diced potatoes, onion, salt, and pepper.

2. Fry until brown and crisp. You may choose to let it stay in large chunks or just keep stirring it, breaking it up.

3. Taste and season as necessary. The corned beef is going to be salty, so make you sure to taste it before adding too much salt.

Yields 2 servings.

Berry Breakfast Cake

- Oil for Dutch oven
- 2 cups all-purpose flour
- ½ cup granulated sugar
- 1 cup fresh or reconstituted buttermilk
- ½ cup butter, melted
- 1 egg or the equivalent of reconstituted powdered egg
- 1½ cups berries

1. Grease a Dutch oven and preheat over medium fire.

2. Mix the flour and sugar in a bowl, then add the buttermilk, butter, and egg.

3. Gently fold in the berries just enough to moisten them. Don't stir too much, or you'll smash the berries and make the cake tough.

4. Pour the batter into the Dutch oven, and bake covered for 20 minutes. When a knife inserted in the center comes out clean, the cake is done.

Yields about 6 servings.

Day-Old Bread Pudding

Survival cooking is all about cooking stick-to-your-ribs food without wasting anything. This recipe will do just that, and it's delicious, too!

- 5 eggs or the equivalent of reconstituted powdered eggs
- 2 cans fresh milk or reconstituted powdered milk (or substitute 1 cup milk for 1 cup heavy cream)
- 2 tablespoons butter, melted
- 2 tablespoons ground allspice
- 1 tablespoon vanilla extract
- 1 loaf dense, day-old bread such as Italian, cut or torn into cubes
- 1 cup raisins

1. Preheat a Dutch oven over medium fire.

2. Beat the eggs in a medium bowl and whip in the milk until combined. Add the melted butter, allspice, and vanilla.

3. Put the bread into the Dutch oven, and pour the egg and milk mixture over it along with the raisins. Mix until the bread is moistened.

4. Cover and bake for 45 minutes or until the bread pudding is no longer soggy.

Yields about 8 servings.

Soups, Roasts, and Stews

One of the easiest and least resource-consuming ways to feed a group of people is to make a nice pot of stew or soup. It's filling and nutritious, and it uses only a few dishes. All you really need is a Dutch oven or a large pot and a ladle.

Dutch Oven Roast

You can make this roast with just about any red meat, including beef, venison, bison, elk, moose, or any other game. If you use wild game, be sure to take the blue membrane off the roast prior to cooking to remove the gamey flavor. Also, if you'd like to make this using canned veggies, just wait to add them until the last 40 minutes or so; that way, they don't turn to mush.

- 2 tablespoons oil or butter
- 4 pounds rump or shoulder roast
- 1 teaspoon salt
- 1 tablespoon black pepper
- 6 fresh or canned potatoes, wedged or cubed
- 8 large carrots, not peeled, cut into 1-inch slices
- 2 medium onions, peeled and quartered
- 2 cups water or beef broth
- 3 tablespoons red wine (optional)
- 2 sprigs fresh rosemary or 1 tablespoon dried
- 2 sprigs fresh thyme or 1 tablespoon dried

1. Heat the Dutch oven over medium fire and add the oil.

2. Salt and pepper the roast.

3. Toss the potatoes, carrots, and onions into the hot oil to brown them, then remove them. Add the meat and brown it on both sides, then remove it.

4. Deglaze the Dutch oven with the water or broth (or if you have it, throw in the red wine). Scrape all of that brown goodness off the bottom of the pan.

5. Add the meat and veggies back in along with the herbs. Cover and cook for about 3 hours.

Yields about 6 servings.

Venison Stew

Again, you can use any red meat that you'd like. The venison just makes this extra delicious.

- 1 quart canned carrots
- 1 quart canned sweet potatoes, cubed
- 1 pint canned green beans
- 1 pint canned corn
- 1 pint canned okra
- 1 quart beef broth or 4 bouillon cubes and 1 pint water
- Salt and pepper to taste
- 1 quart canned venison
- ¼ cup all-purpose flour, arrowroot powder, or cornstarch

1. Add all the ingredients except the meat and flour into a Dutch oven over medium fire. Don't waste the liquid that the veggies were canned in—use it as liquid in the stew to flavor it. Cook at a rolling boil for 30 minutes.

2. Add the flour to the meat, and toss to coat. Add to the stew mix, and simmer for another 15 minutes so that the stew thickens.

3. Let set for 10 minutes to cool, and serve.

Yields about 9 servings.

Italian Rustica

- 2 quarts tomato juice
- 1 pint canned carrots, mostly drained
- 1 pint green beans, mostly drained
- 1 pint canned tomatoes, rough chopped, not drained
- 2 stalks celery, chopped
- 1 medium onion, chopped
- 1 teaspoon salt
- 1 teaspoon black pepper
- 1 tablespoon dried oregano
- 2 sprigs of rosemary
- 1 sprig thyme
- 1 bay leaf
- 1 tablespoon chopped or dried oregano
- 2 cups dried pasta (rotini works well)

1. Combine all the ingredients except the pasta in a Dutch oven over medium fire. Bring to a rolling boil for 30 minutes, then add the pasta.

2. Boil for another 20–25 minutes or until the pasta is done.

3. Let it cool for 15 minutes, and enjoy.

Yields about 8 servings.

Ham and Bean Soup

- 2 cups dried northern or cannellini beans
- 2 quarts water
- 1 ham hock (optional)
- 2 teaspoons salt
- 1 tablespoon black pepper
- 2 cups chopped ham

1. Soak the dried beans in water overnight.

2. Drain the beans, and put them in a Dutch oven over medium fire along with 2 quarts of water, the ham hock, salt, and pepper. Cook for 2–3 hours at a rolling boil. Add water as needed to keep everything covered.

3. After the beans have cooked for a couple of hours and are tender, remove the ham hock and add the chopped ham. Cook for 20 more minutes or until ham is hot and broth has thickened a bit.

Yields about 6 servings.

Southwest Stew

- 1 quart canned chicken breast with broth
- 1 cup rice
- 1 large onion, diced, or 3 tablespoons dried onion
- 1 pint diced tomatoes with juice
- 1 can corn
- 1 can black beans, drained
- 1 tablespoon dried cilantro or 2 sprigs fresh cilantro
- 2 packs taco seasoning
- 1 small can green chilies, diced
- 1 quart chicken broth or 1 quart water and 3 chicken bouillon cubes
- 1 teaspoon salt

1. Shred the chicken, and put all the ingredients in a Dutch oven over medium fire.

2. Boil for 1 hour or until the rice is tender.

Yields about 6 servings.

Cabbage Stew

- 1 pound ground meat
- 1 pint canned cabbage, chopped
- 1 large onion, chopped
- 1 pint canned tomatoes, chopped
- ½ cup chopped celery
- 1 (15-ounce) can kidney beans, undrained
- 1 cup water
- 1½ teaspoons salt
- ½ teaspoon black pepper
- ¼ teaspoon garlic powder
- 1 teaspoon chili powder or to taste

1. Brown the meat in a Dutch oven over medium fire and drain.

2. Add the veggies and brown lightly.

3. Add the rest of the ingredients and bring to a boil.

4. Once the stew is boiling, reduce to a simmer and keep simmering until the cabbage is tender and the flavors are melded, about 40 minutes.

Yields about 6 servings.

Chicken Chili

- 1 quart canned chicken breast
- 2 tablespoons oil or melted butter
- 1 medium onion, chopped
- 2 chili peppers, chopped (optional)
- 1 quart canned tomatoes, chopped, with juice
- 2 (15-ounce) cans kidney beans
- 2 tablespoons chili powder or to taste
- 1 teaspoon salt
- 1 teaspoon black pepper

1. Drain and shred the chicken.

2. Add the butter, onions, chili peppers, and chicken to a Dutch oven over medium fire, and cook until browned.

3. Add the rest of the ingredients, and bring to a simmer. Simmer for 1 hour or until the flavors are melded.

Yields about 8 servings.

Chicken Potpie, Country Style

- 1 cup self-rising flour
- ¾ cup fresh milk or reconstituted powdered milk
- 1½ teaspoons salt, divided
- 1 quart canned chicken, deboned, with broth
- 2 chicken bouillon cubes
- 1 pint canned peas
- 1 pint canned sliced carrots
- ½ teaspoon black pepper

1. Mix the flour, milk, and ½ teaspoon of the salt in a small bowl and set aside. It should be a slurry. If not, add a bit more milk.

2. Brown the chicken in a Dutch oven over medium fire, then add the broth and deglaze the pan. Dissolve the bouillon cubes in the broth. Put the chicken back in, and add the peas, carrots, 1 teaspoon of salt, and pepper.

3. Pour the flour slurry over the top of the chicken mixture, and bake for 30 minutes or until it's bubbly and the biscuit topping is brown.

Yields about 4 servings.

Beef Stew

- 4 pounds beef tips
- ½ cup all-purpose flour
- 1 medium onion, chopped
- 1 pint canned sliced carrots
- 2 cups diced celery
- 2 cups water
- 2 teaspoons salt
- 1 teaspoon black pepper
- 1 teaspoon dried rosemary
- 1 teaspoon dried tarragon
- 1 pint canned potatoes or 4 fresh potatoes, cubed
- 1 pint canned tomatoes, chopped
- 1 bay leaf

1. Toss the beef tips in the flour, then cook the beef, onions, carrots, and celery in a Dutch oven over medium fire until the beef is rare but browned on all sides.

2. Add the water and seasonings, and simmer for 1–2 hours or until the meat is tender.

3. Add the potatoes, tomatoes, and bay leaf, and return to a simmer until the veggies are tender.

4. Remove from the heat, remove the bay leaf, and allow to rest for 10 minutes.

Yields about 6 servings.

Cajun Fish Stew

This can be made with any chicken, fish, or seafood that you have available.

- 1 canned ham, diced
- 2 stalks celery, diced
- 1 medium onion, diced
- 1 quart canned tomatoes, chopped
- 1 pint canned okra
- 1 tablespoon garlic powder
- 1 tablespoon hot sauce or to taste
- 1 tablespoon Worcestershire sauce
- Salt to taste
- 6 trout fillets, cut into chunks
- 2 teaspoons of gumbo filé powder or 1 tablespoon all-purpose flour mixed with ¼ cup water and 1 teaspoon Cajun seasoning

1. Sauté the ham, celery, and onion in a Dutch oven over medium fire until soft.

2. Add the tomatoes, okra (with the water it's canned in), garlic powder, hot sauce, Worcestershire sauce, and a bit more water if needed. Bring to a boil and taste. Add salt if needed.

3. Add the fish chunks and boil until they're tender, about 15 minutes. Add the filé powder or the flour slurry and Cajun seasoning. Stir well and remove from heat. Allow to sit for 10 minutes and serve.

Yields about 4 servings.

Quick Meals and Sides

Poor Man's Skillet

Nutritious, quick, and tasty, this meal doesn't take much effort and is made of simple, readily available ingredients.

- 2 pounds ground beef or venison
- 1 small onion, chopped
- ½ teaspoon salt
- ½ teaspoon black pepper
- 3 fresh potatoes or 1 pint canned potatoes, cubed
- 1 pint canned green beans, drained
- 1 (15-ounce) can tomato soup or canned creamed tomatoes

1. Brown the ground beef, onion, salt, and pepper in a large iron skillet over medium fire.

2. Add the potatoes and cook until they're tender and brown.

3. Add the rest of the ingredients and cook until hot.

4. Eat either by itself or with bread if you have it.

Yields about 4 servings.

Dried Beef Gravy and Potatoes

If you'd like to make this a breakfast meal, simply serve it over biscuits and add a fried egg or two on top of the entire dish. It's also great to eat either alone or over bread or biscuits.

- ¼ cup butter or bacon grease
- 1 pint canned potatoes or 4 fresh potatoes, diced
- ½ teaspoon salt or to taste
- ½ teaspoon black pepper or to taste

- ¼ cup all-purpose flour
- 1½ cups water
- 1 cup fresh milk or reconstituted powdered milk
- 1 pint jar dried beef

1. Melt the butter in an iron skillet over medium fire. Toss in the potatoes, salt, and pepper, and brown. Be careful not to add too much salt because the dried beef is salty.

2. Sprinkle the flour over the potatoes and stir until it starts to brown. Add the water slowly and stir. It will get thick at first, but stir well before adding more water so that you don't get lumps. Add the milk.

3. Add the dried beef and allow to simmer slowly for 5 minutes. If it's too thick, add a bit more water or milk.

Yields about 4 servings.

Ramen Noodle Stir-Fry

This is a quick, easy recipe to make, and ramen is inexpensive, lasts practically forever, and should be a part of your emergency food supply.

- 2 packs oriental- or chicken-flavored ramen noodles
- ½ small onion, sliced
- 1 large can or 2 small cans chunk chicken
- 1 pint canned peas
- 1 pint canned green beans
- 1 small can mushrooms or ¼ cup dried mushrooms
- 1 fresh red bell pepper, chopped (optional)
- 1 tablespoon low-sodium soy sauce

1. Boil the ramen noodles per the package's instructions without adding the seasoning packs. Drain.

2. While you're waiting for the noodles to cook, brown the onion in a large iron skillet over medium fire.

3. Add the chicken, peas, green beans, mushrooms, and bell pepper, if you're using it. Heat them up, and then add the ramen noodles, seasoning from the ramen packs, and soy sauce. (Using low-sodium soy sauce prevents the need of excess water.) Stir just enough to mix and reheat the ramen.

Yields about 4 servings.

Quick Venison

- Oil for skillet
- 1 teaspoon salt
- 1 teaspoon black pepper
- 3 pounds venison steaks, sliced 1-inch thick
- ¾ cup water
- 1 (10-ounce) can cream of mushroom soup
- 2 beef bouillon cubes
- 1 tablespoon dried onion

1. Preheat a large, greased iron skillet over medium fire. Rub the salt and pepper on the steaks, and sear in the skillet until they're cooked the way you like them. Remove and set aside.

2. Deglaze the skillet with the water, then add the rest of the ingredients. Bring to a quick simmer and remove from the fire.

3. Place the steaks on a plate, and ladle the gravy over them.

Yields about 5 servings.

Sweet Lemon-Pepper Chicken and Rice

- ½ cup all-purpose flour
- 1 tablespoon lemon-pepper seasoning
- ½ teaspoon salt
- 1 quart canned chicken breast with broth
- 1 cup water (optional)
- 2 cups instant rice
- 2 tablespoons butter or vegetable oil
- 1 tablespoon honey mixed with 1 tablespoon water

---

1. Combine the flour, lemon-pepper seasoning, and salt. Drain the chicken broth into a medium saucepan and add water if necessary to make 2 cups. Bring to a boil and add the rice. Follow the instant rice cooking directions.

2. Preheat a large iron skillet with the butter or oil in it.

3. Drizzle the honey water over the chicken breasts, and toss gently to coat. Roll each breast in the flour mixture, and place gently into the skillet. Fry on both sides until chicken is done and browned.

4. Serve the chicken over the rice.

Yields about 4 servings.

Whitefish Balls

- 4 trout or other whitefish fillets, skinned and minced
- ¼ cup cooked oatmeal
- ¼ teaspoon salt
- ½ teaspoon lemon-pepper seasoning
- 1 egg or equivalent of reconstituted powdered egg
- 2 tablespoons butter or oil

1. Combine the fish, oatmeal, salt, lemon-pepper seasoning, and egg in a bowl, and mix well.

2. Preheat a large iron skillet with the butter or oil in it over medium fire.

3. Roll the fish mixture into 1½-inch balls and place them in the hot skillet. Brown each side of the balls well.

4. Remove from the heat and place on a plate. Serve immediately.

Yields about 15 balls.

Curried Rice

This is a great side dish to carry with you in your pack. You can mix up the dry ingredients, and put single servings in resealable plastic bags. Otherwise, make it as directed.

- 2 cups water
- 2 chicken bouillon cubes
- 2 cups instant rice
- 1 tablespoon curry powder
- 1 teaspoon garlic powder
- ¼ tablespoon granulated sugar
- ½ teaspoon salt

1. Bring the water and bouillon cubes to a boil in a Dutch oven over medium fire and remove from the fire.

2. Add all the other ingredients and cover.

3. Let sit covered for 5 minutes or until the rice is tender.

Yields 4 servings.

Savory Sweet Potato Wedges

- 2 fresh or canned sweet potatoes
- 1 tablespoon oil
- 1 teaspoon salt
- 1 teaspoon black pepper
- 1 teaspoon dried rosemary
- Oil for skillet

---

1. Cut the sweet potatoes into wedges, and put them in a bowl. Drizzle the oil over them, and sprinkle with the salt, pepper, and rosemary. Toss to combine.

2. Preheat a greased iron skillet over medium fire. Fry the wedges, browning on each side until tender. Remove from the heat and serve immediately.

Yields 4 servings.

Fried Cabbage

- 1 quart canned cabbage
- 1 cup cubed canned ham
- 1 medium onion, sliced
- ½ teaspoon salt
- 1 teaspoon black pepper

1. Preheat a greased iron skillet over medium fire.

2. Add all the ingredients and fry until the cabbage and onions are tender.

Yields about 6 servings.

Sourdough Starter

A sourdough starter is a survivalist's best friend; from it, you can make myriad delicious breads and dessert recipes. It doesn't require yeast, and if you keep it going, you can use the same starter for years.

• 2 cups all-purpose flour	• 2½ cups lukewarm water

1. Put the flour in a glass container. Add the water and stir together until mixed. Cover mixture with a towel and set it in a warm place. Make sure that it isn't too hot and there aren't any drafts that will chill the mixture.

2. In 4–6 days, you'll notice that it's bubbling and smelling wonderfully yeasty. It's now ready. Keep it going by stirring in 2 cups of flour and about ¾ cup of lukewarm water whenever you use a cup of the starter.

Yields 1 batch of starter.

Personal Hygiene Items

It may seem now that if you're in a survival situation, you won't be worrying much about smelling good. That may be true for the first few days. After that, however, the niceties will become luxuries to you. If you talk to survivors of great disasters or war, they will tell you that often even small amounts of deodorant, shampoo, or toothpaste were more valuable than food.

Although you probably won't have access to many of these ingredients post-disaster, they're great to make and keep in your emergency supply for both personal use and for barter. They're all chemical-free and actually good for you, so making your own is just one more way to be healthier and less dependent upon commercial substances.

You'll note that coconut oil is a key component in several of these, and though it's a little expensive, its health benefits are amazing. Since it has antibacterial and antimicrobial properties, it's a great base for many personal hygiene products. Use organic, unrefined oil when possible. If you don't want the coconut smell, use expeller-pressed oil so it doesn't lose its efficacy through heating.

Deodorant

Coconut oil hovers between liquid and solid at room temperature, so it will probably be a bit liquid once you start working with it. That's normal. Although this isn't an antiperspirant, once you wear it for a while and your body becomes accustomed to not depending on chemical inhibitors, you'll notice that you won't produce as much underarm sweat.

- ¼ cup arrowroot powder or cornstarch
- ¼ cup baking soda
- 7 tablespoons coconut oil, approximately

1. Combine the arrowroot and baking soda, and then add the coconut oil 1 tablespoon at a time until a nice thick paste forms, similar to store-bought deodorant.

2. Store in a jar or other container, and just smooth a teaspoon or two under each armpit.

Yields about 1 cup.

Body Lotion Bars

These are similar to bars of soap, but when you rub it on your skin, it leaves a nice layer of moisturizer. Feel free to add essential oils for health or scent properties. These have a nice coconut, nutty scent just the way they are.

- ⅓ cup coconut oil
- ⅓ cup shea, mango, cocoa, kokum, or illipe butter, or any combination of these
- ⅓ cup beeswax
- 1 teaspoon vitamin E oil
- A few drops of essential oil (optional)

1. Line a muffin pan with parchment paper, or use mini loaf pans lined with plastic wrap or parchment paper. You could also use soap molds or basically any kind of container you'd like to use to shape these bars.

2. Combine all the ingredients except the essential oils in a glass canning jar, and place it in a pan of warm water. Heat over medium fire until the water is starting to simmer, and then remove from the heat. Stir mixture and let it warm to the point of melting. When liquefied, stir well and then add the essential oil.

3. Pour into your molds and allow to cool completely before removing. Store in resealable plastic bags or airtight plastic containers.

4. When you want to use a lotion bar, just run it over your skin for a nice layer of moisturizing lotion.

Yields about 3 bars, using muffin tins filled halfway.

Antiseptic Ointment

This ointment is all-natural and has antibacterial, antifungal, antibiotic, antiviral, and analgesic properties.

- 2 ounces beeswax, softened
- 1 cup coconut or almond oil
- ½ teaspoon tea tree oil
- ½ teaspoon vitamin E oil
- 1 ounce jojoba oil
- 24 drops lavender essential oil
- 12 drops lemon essential oil

1. Combine all the ingredients, warming slightly to liquefy the mixture so the oils meld.

2. Store in an airtight tin or jar, and use on cuts, skin irritations, or any other condition that requires a salve.

Yields about 1½ cups.

Soothing Sunscreen Lip Balm

- 3 tablespoons coconut oil
- 3 drops tea tree oil
- 3 drops lemon oil
- 1 tablespoon shea butter

1. Combine all the ingredients and store in an airtight tin in a cool, dry place. Apply as often as necessary.

Yields about 3 tablespoons.

Homemade Toothpaste

Many people don't know it, but salt is one of the best disinfectants you can use. It also helps remove food particles and buildup from your teeth.

- ⅓ cup baking soda
- 1 teaspoon unrefined sea salt

- 1 teaspoon peppermint extract to taste (or spearmint, cinnamon, etc.)
- About 2 tablespoons water

1. Combine baking soda, salt, and extract with enough water to create the consistency of toothpaste.

2. Store in an airtight tin or jar. Use like regular toothpaste.

Yields about ½ cup.

CONCLUSION

In a survival situation, how you get things done won't be nearly as important as getting them done. Fancy pots, difficult-to-make intricate recipes, and commercial hair products will be replaced with iron skillets, Dutch ovens, and whatever food and hygiene products you have stored or that you can make yourself from your supplies.

Advance preparation will be crucial to giving you a fighting chance of making it through a disaster, even if it's for only a few days. Stocking foodstuffs that don't spoil easily, don't need refrigeration, and can be used in many different ways will make your life infinitely easier.

Canning is a great way to preserve foods without worrying about chemicals and excess sodium. It's also inexpensive, especially if you're fortunate enough to be able to grow your own foods. Virtually any individual food or recipe can be canned, too, so having some of your favorite meals already preserved, cooked, and ready to eat will really make life without power or other modern conveniences a little easier to bear. One can live happily on plain canned tuna for only so long.

Other items that are extremely useful to keep stocked include herbs and spices, both for seasoning and medicinal purposes. Consider buying a book specifically about the various uses of herbs and keep it nearby.

Thanks for reading and using this book, and we hope that you found the information interesting and useful. If you're fortunate, you'll never need either the information or the emergency supply, but it's much better to be prepared than not to be!

ALTITUDE CHART

Below are altitudes of selected cities in the United States and Canada. To find the exact altitude of your location, use the search features on the EarthTools website (www.earthtools.org).

STATE	CITY	FEET	METERS
ARIZONA	Mesa	1,243	379
	Phoenix	1,150	351
	Scottsdale	1,257	383
	Tucson	2,389	728
CALIFORNIA	Fontana	1,237	377
	Moreno Valley	1,631	497
COLORADO	Aurora	5,471	1,668
	Colorado Springs	6,010	1,832
	Denver	5,183	1,580
GEORGIA	Atlanta	1,026	313
IDAHO	Boise	2,730	832
	Idaho Falls	4,705	1,434
IOWA	Sioux City	1,201	366
KANSAS	Wichita	1,299	396
MONTANA	Billings	3,123	952
	Missoula	3,209	978
NEBRASKA	Lincoln	1,176	358
	Omaha	1,090	332
NEVADA	Henderson	1,867	569
	Las Vegas	2,001	610
	Reno	4,505	1,373
NEW MEXICO	Albuquerque	5,312	1,619
	Santa Fe	7,260	2,213
NORTH CAROLINA	Asheville	2,134	650
NORTH DAKOTA	Bismarck	1,686	514
OHIO	Akron	1,004	306
OKLAHOMA	Oklahoma City	1,201	366
PENNSYLVANIA	Pittsburgh	1,370	418
SOUTH DAKOTA	Rapid City	3,202	976
TEXAS	Amarillo	3,605	1,099
	El Paso	3,740	1,140
	Lubbock	3,256	992
UTAH	Provo	4,551	1,387
	Salt Lake City	4,226	1,288
WASHINGTON	Spokane	1,843	562
WYOMING	Casper	5,150	1,570

PROVINCE	CITY	FEET	METERS
ALBERTA	Calgary	3,600	1,100
ALBERTA	Edmonton	2,201	671
ONTARIO	Hamilton	1,063	324
MANITOBA	Brandon	1,343	409
SASKATCHEWAN	Regina	1,893	577
SASKATCHEWAN	Saskatoon	1,580	482

BUG-OUT BAG CHECKLIST

Prepper's Checklist — Bug-Out Bag

- ☐ Aluminum foil
- ☐ Can opener
- ☐ Cash, coins
- ☐ Compass
- ☐ Deck of cards
- ☐ Docs box (your vital documents)
- ☐ Duct tape
- ☐ Fire kit
- ☐ First aid kit
- ☐ Flashlight, extra batteries
- ☐ Food and water to last at least 3 days
- ☐ Map of local area
- ☐ Medications
- ☐ Mess kit
- ☐ Multi-function knife
- ☐ Multi-use shovel
- ☐ Pants/shorts, shirt, socks, shoes, jacket
- ☐ Paracord
- ☐ Radios (2-way) with batteries
- ☐ Space blanket
- ☐ Sunscreen
- ☐ Tarp
- ☐ Water purification tabs
- ☐ Whistle

INDEX

Printed in Great Britain
by Amazon

54948961R00138